AF265730

Art Speaks,
The Catalogue

An Anthology of Artwork and
Ekphrastic Writing
by the CNY Branch of the NLAPW

Also by
the CNY Branch of the NLAPW

In the Company of Women,
An Anthology Commemorating the
90th Anniversary of the CNY Branch of the
NLAPW

Edited by Lorraine Arsenault and
Nancy A. Dafoe

MLMG Designs, © 2016

Correspondence to
mlgardner37@yahoo.com
or
dafoe.nancy@gmail.com

Art Speaks,

The Catalogue

An Anthology of Artwork and Ekphrastic Writing by the CNY Branch of the NLAPW

Edited by Nancy Avery Dafoe

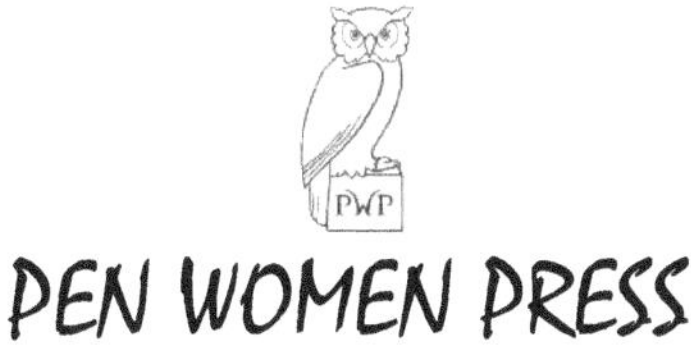

PEN WOMEN PRESS

Cover design: Lucy Arnold
Cover art: Linda Bigness
Pen Women Press Book Coordinator: Lucy Arnold
Edited by Nancy Avery Dafoe

ISBN 978-1-950251-06-3 (paperback)

For book information, address the editor at
dafoe.nancy@gmail.com or
contact@nancydafoebooks.com

First Edition
Printed in the United States of America.

Published by the
National League of American Pen Women, Inc.
PEN WOMEN PRESS

Founded in 1897, the National League of American Pen Women, Inc. is a nonprofit dedicated to promoting the arts. NLAPW, Inc. 1300 17th Street, NW, Washington, D.C. 20036-1973; www.nlapw.org

At the Core, the Legacy

In the matter of our personal lives,
we have only that which we are given –
a lifetime, however brief or long,
to claim our gifts, hone them, set them free
unburdened from doubt, resolved to share them
and inspire others to nurture their own.

In the matter of our ninety-five years,
we have only that which we have been given –
the remarkable gifts of those gone before
and what we make of the present time
as creative women engaged in the world,
celebrating our history and our gifts,

being mindful of the pivotal place of the arts
in the public square and a thriving nation.
This is our legacy and, yes,
at the core of who we are.

Mary L. Gardner

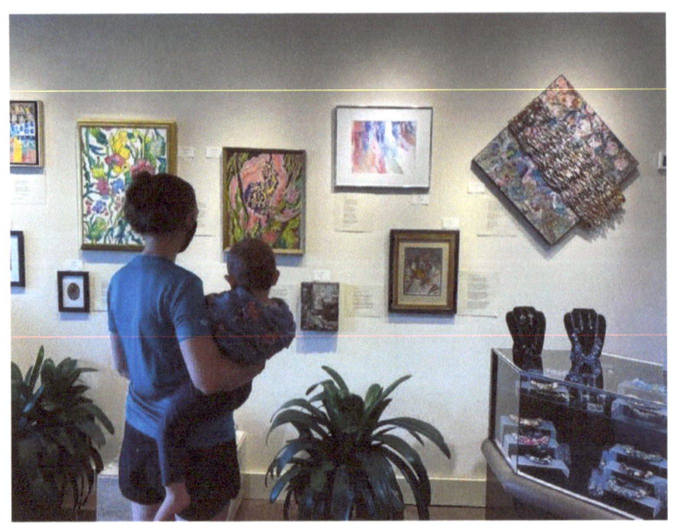

*Photo of visitors to the Edgewood Gallery exhibition
"Art Speaks," by Pen Woman Janine M. DeBaise.*

Acknowledgements

Members of the Central New York (CNY) Branch of the NLAPW offer our deeply felt thank you to Cheryl Chappell, owner of the Edgewood Gallery in Syracuse, NY; to Donna Lamb, Executive Director of the Schweinfurth Art Center in Auburn, NY; Davana Robedee, Program Director at the Schweinfurth Art Center; and Maria Welych, Marketing Director at the Schweinfurth for helping to coordinate the art exhibitions inviting our ekphrastic responses.

Special thank you to and appreciation for all of the "Made in New York" artists whose work inspired Pen Women to write.

Contents

1

Ekphrastic Reponses to the "Art Speaks" Exhibition at the Edgewood Gallery, 2021

Introduction

The Central New York (CNY) Branch of the National League of American Pen Women (NLAPW) produced *Art Speaks, The Catalogue* in commemoration of their 95th anniversary year. This anthology derives from two exhibitions and ekphrastic readings in 2021. Pen Women engage in conversation and information sharing around their respective endeavors in the arts and find this a core value of membership in the organization.

The "Art Speaks" exhibition at the Edgewood Gallery in Syracuse, NY (July 2-August 13, 2021) featured artists and writers from the CNY Branch. The exhibition presented twenty works of art and twenty ekphrastic poems; that is, poetry created in response to what the art evokes in the poet's imagination or recall. Ekphrastic response need not employ descriptive language nor attempt to imagine what might have been in the artist's mind. Works of art and responsive poems were hung beside one another. The show was a type of creative conversation among artists and poets that offered viewers two avenues to interact with each work. *Art Speaks, The Catalog*, in its design and layout, encourages readers to take advantage of the opportunity to interact with the art in multiple ways.

In recent years, the CNY Branch has presented three readings of ekphrastic poetry inspired by works of art in the *Made in New York* show, a signature annual event at the Schweinfurth Art Center in Auburn, NY. Included in this anthology are a number of poetry and art pairings from the 2021 *Made in New York* exhibition.

The National League of American Pen Women was formed in October 1897 when women journalists were refused admittance to the National Press Club. Founding members included women writers, journalists, and lecturers, many prominent in their respective fields. The CNY Branch was formally admitted to the National League on October 1, 1926 and convened in the Hotel Onondaga in Syracuse, New York.

Today, the League includes 60 branches and more than 1,200 members. Membership expanded over the years to embrace women artists, composers, choreographers, and women in the allied arts. The central mission of NLAPW remains the same: to encourage and recognize the work of professional standards in letters, visual and other creative arts, and provide opportunities for members to inspire and encourage one another, as well as their communities.

Judith McGinn, President   Mary Gardner
NLAPW, CNY Branch   Chair, "Art Speaks"

Pen Women Artists in the "Art Speaks" Exhibition at the Edgewood Gallery, 2021

(Pen Women artists' work in order of first appearance)

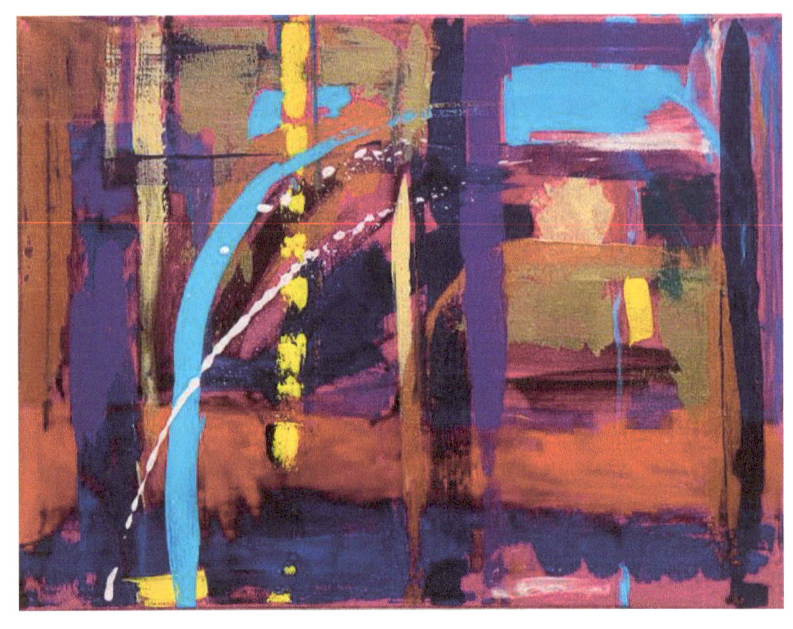

"Through the Open Door" by Wendy Harris

If Only Blue Could Suffice

If only blue were enough to unlock mystery,
the way it anchors a wave below its crest,
sturdies a door, or the window taking in the sky.

Blue pillow of sleep, come this way,
where peace lies, the solace you have been waiting
to collect. Through this door, find the red pulse

of each of your dawns. Noon's startling sun,
grapes and berries, honey to soothe your throat.
Sing. Follow the way, through the door, beyond

the limits of threshold into simple bliss, a warranted
dream, the law of rest keeping doubt and fear at bay.
Blue is the silent confirmation that all is well,

at least for the moment. Surrender. Surely you will rise.
You will start again, moving through another day,
clutching the gold key in your palm, deep in your pocket.

Georgia A. Popoff

A Universe Chock Full of Hearts

Deep within the body of each atom
beats an infinitesimal heart, sparks flashing,
the electric pulse discovered in our wrists.

Hearts huddle among the clouds, conspiring
to rain. The birthplace of rainbows, first
inkling of lightning. Sometimes a golden threat.

Within the chest's cavern, a persistent red
muscle pushes its clever little thump
to the surface, like a Big Ben alarm clock

quietly ticking in the corner, waiting to be wound.
A simple twist of the wrist guarantees more time.
Hope itself. The embodiment of trust in the face

of an imperfect existence. There is life, posing
as heart, where the best of us rally. We surpass
our fears and revel in the comfort that we are here.

Georgia A. Popoff

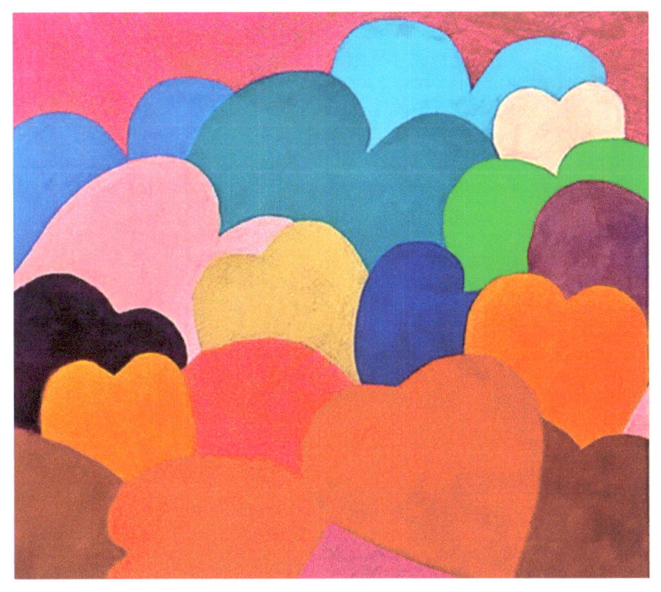

"Heart of Gold" by Wendy Harris

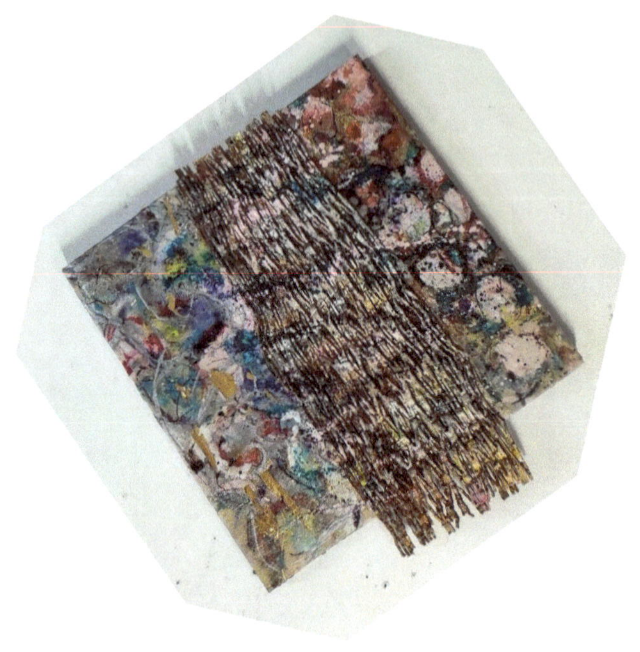

"Woven Thoughts" by Linda Bigness

Just before dawn

When dark night anxieties swirl,
I reach inside my head
to untangle each silken strand of stress,
those familiar snarled knots
I unclench my teeth, relax my jaw
Breathe, breathe, breathe

My dream fingers brush
and sweep, combing smooth
each churning thought, each seething worry
I pull the blanket over my head,
warmth falling like water
Breathe, breathe, breathe

I comb out brooding snakes,
rusted fragments of regret,
bubbles of self-doubt
weaving thoughts into plaits
until I fall asleep
beneath the weight

Janine M. DeBaise

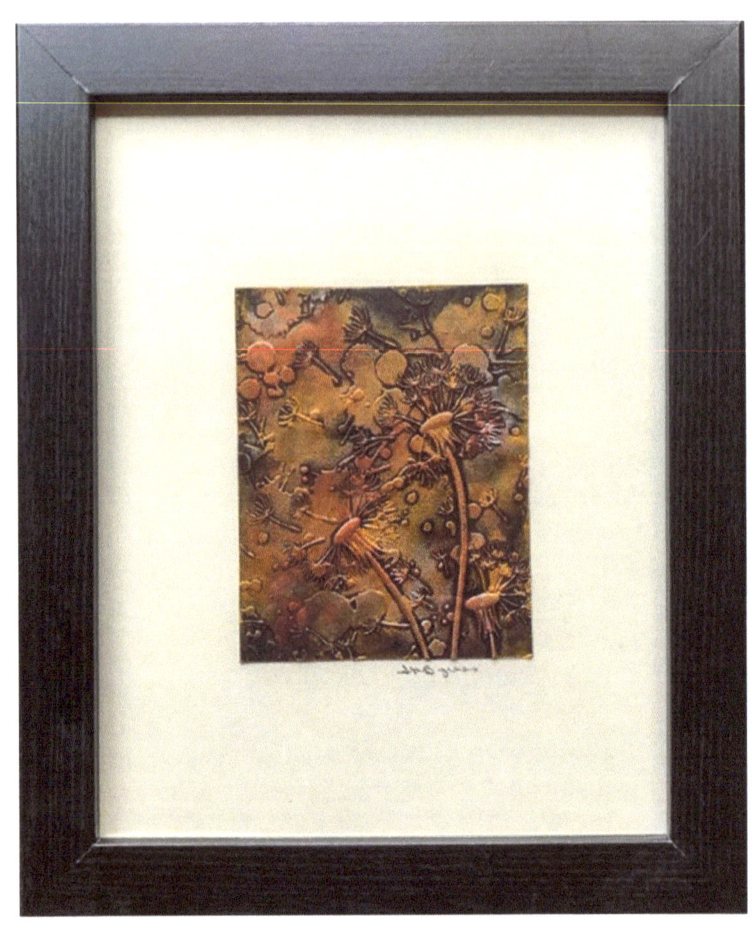

"Blowing in the Wind" by Sheila M. Byrnes

Breath

my father stoops to choose a dandelion
his gnarled hands shake
heart pumping blood through narrowed arteries
with a warning swish the doctor hears

in childhood we had so many wishes
we could squander them
we puffed dandelion seeds across grassy hills
floated them into sunshine

what do you wish for at ninety?
one last summer on the river
hoisting canvas to sky
napping under ancient oak trees

glimpses of your wife
those rare moments
when she emerges from dementia
like an island in mist

all I know at sixty
are the things I cannot ask for
turning back time
escaping mortality

not enough dandelions
no god big enough

Janine M. DeBaise

Clothesline Lessons

Winds whip towels,
sheets dance on wisps of air,
sunshine's perfume infuses the scene
and I remember…
helping my mother lug the basket to the yard
to hang the wash, handing her clothespins,
washcloths, and the baby's shirts.
Later returning to help put pins away, fold,
then breathe in the fresh sun-borne scent
and my mother's love.

Housewife work, her daily job,
never ending, never complaining.
She, who loved to read, knew poems by heart,
who once sat in gifted classes with talented teachers,
now cooked, cleaned, sewed, put away, made a home.

In my day, I, who never hung the wash,
only cooked sort of, barely sewed,
never made pies,
find myself drawn to paintings
of Maine's colorful clotheslines,
full of laundry drying in open air.
As if from these paintings, I will find answers
for living, raising children, tending a home.
As if regret for not being grateful enough
for clean laundry straight from the line
would be enough to thank my mother for her sacrifice.
As if I could figure out if it really is possible
to have it all?

Janet Clare Fagal

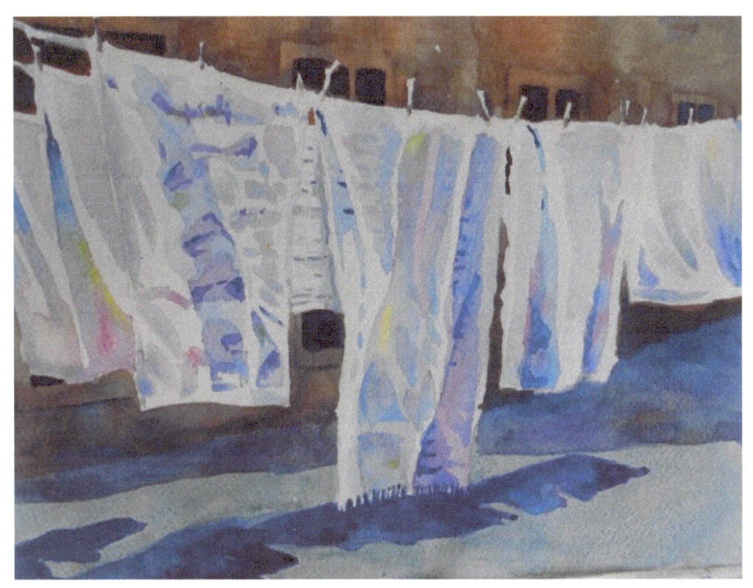

"White Wash" by Susan Murphy

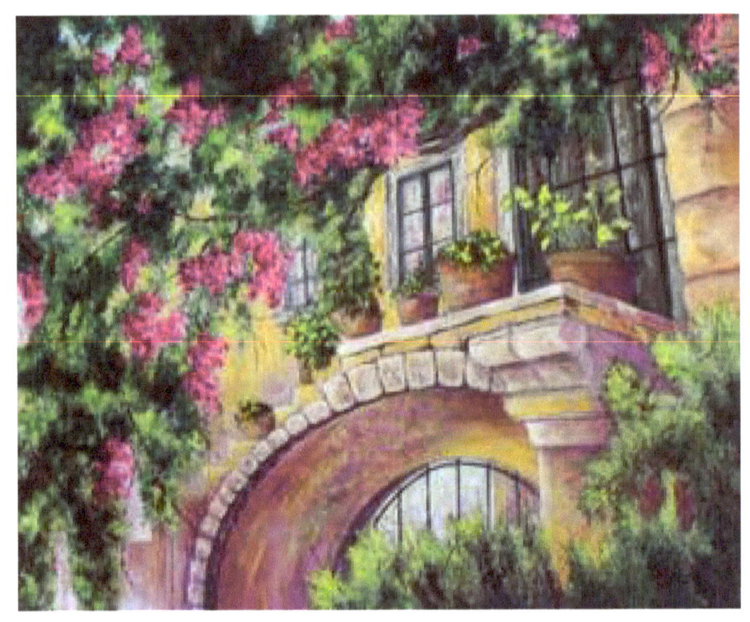

"Afternoon Sun, Crete" by Joan Applebaum

Family Reunion

Long ago in Tuscany,
or maybe it was Crete,
my grandparents visited relatives.
In a box of old papers,
I find photos, faded scenes from a party.
No names or dates
or where they were taken.
I see happiness everywhere.
This family of young and old
gathers round garden tables
overflowing with salads, pasta,
wine and fruit.
They share stories.
Heads tipped back in laughter,
hands upturned and waving,
as if their words are dancing.
Campagna, famiglia, amore, *
it's all there…
where the sun's rays cast delicate shadows
on stucco walls, and pink blossoms
like lacey mantillas drape themselves
in the sweetness of summer-scented air.
My Nonna tucks a flower behind her ear,
bends her head as if in prayer,
grasps a woman's hands and smiles.
Molto bene, I can hear her say.
Indeed, *molto bene,*
molto bene. **

Janet Clare Fagal

*Countryside, family, love
**Very good

The Fountain

Walking into an old master's palette,
I stop at *The Fountain*, pigments radiating
warmth of a Tuscan courtyard in summer,

where I reach to quench my fresh thirst,
dipping fingers into cobalt teal-tinged
water that has assumed hue of aging bronze.

Heat of the colors generous but not dry,
because a Venetian red *brocca* endlessly pours
itself into a transparent earth-yellow urn

with a spout opening into another urn
filling slowly until cobalt blue and white brush-
strokes from a mullion-sectioned window

remind the eye of the ways in which color
moves the mind, and rectangles and circles
set us down across from sun's shadows

in the shade of potted citrus plant on which
a single lemon hangs low over plaster wall,
allowing bittersweet scent of Italian countryside.

Artist creating another time, another place
for a woman walking through an exhibition
where the precise moment of her past emerges.

Nancy Avery Dafoe

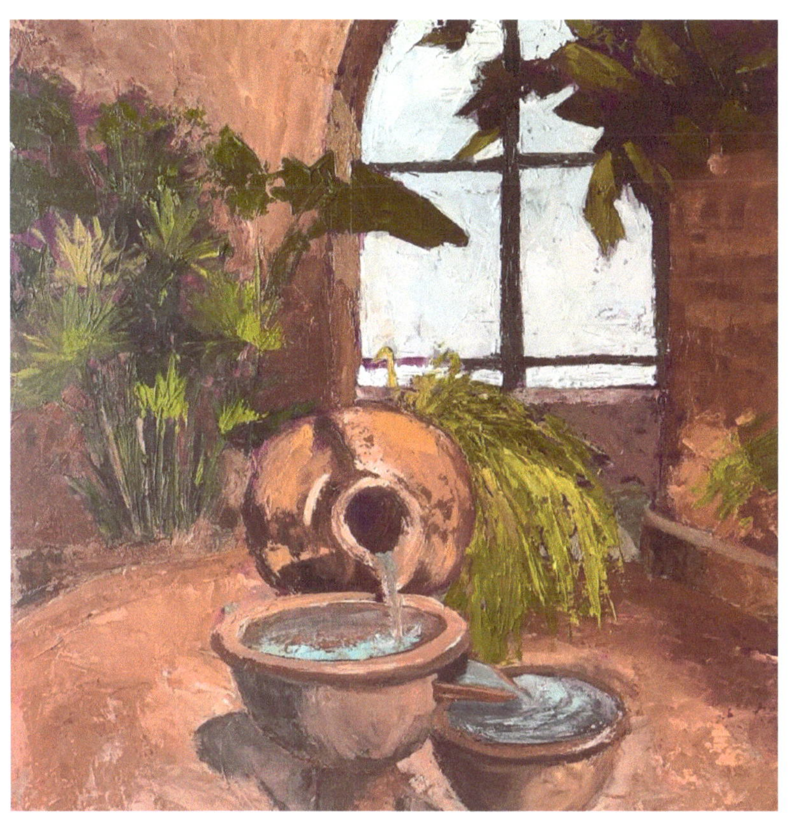

"The Fountain" by Patty Mabie

Time Traveler

The ancient folio remains closed until a monk
uncovers it and donates the text to a library
where its antiquarian pages are opened.
Retrieval of what has come before, our history,
our written words, our knowledge woven like threads
of string theory, entrance only a possibility
until a librarian examines where we've been.

Nothing pristine about its story or fragile pages
darkened by time, like losses of memories
no longer accessible. "The condition renders it
worthless," says the expert. "See here, where back
strip has broken, plating is rubbed away, pages
exposed to moisture, the curling of paper?
Like people, books are sensitive to heat and damp.
And, it has been stored on its side, damaging spine.
You can see browning, and, development
of mold. No care was taken to preserve it."

After the expert leaves, the librarian pulls on gloves
to leaf through old paper, amazed at the colors,
some made from toxic mercury sulfide; Egyptian
blue still beautiful. Then she begins reading
another language, everything else falling away.
She deciphers slowly at first, past not so different
from our present. She smiles then weeps
with discoveries. We are destined not to retain
our memories, our joys, or our lives, but
there is this—this worn and misused testament:
ancient book, time traveler, holding our record.

Nancy Avery Dafoe

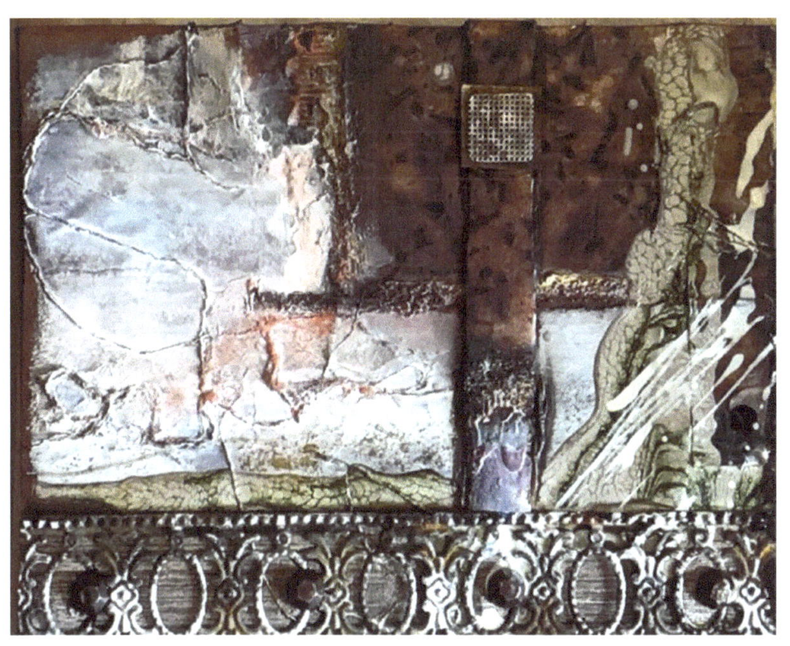

"The Ancient Book" by Mary Raineri

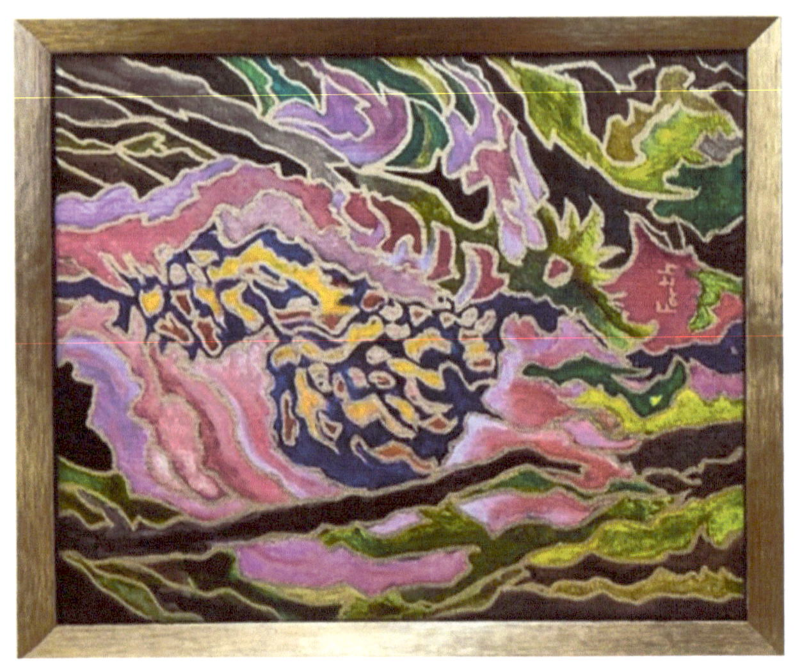

"Botanical Musing" by Marilyn Forth

Musing on Botanicals

How does your garden grow?
the artist asks, setting before us a
veritable Eden of blooms and buds,
vines, tendrils, and fanciful notions of leaf
exulting in their diversity, their beauty
rendered flawless in her skillful hand.

How does your garden grow?
the artist asks, and the poet responds:
Ah! Let us take heart in nature's scheme –
warming earth, sun and rain, hint of leaf,
a packet of sage advice to plant when
all danger of frost is past. Not unlike
lines, archived words, unfolding themes
held fast in the cycling ways of the Muse,
falling into place, slow growing.

How does your garden grow? God asks.
The frost has long since passed.
I have sent you sun and rain,
seeds and roots to sow and scatter
as you will and nurture as you can.
Enjoy and wonder at the beauty of it all,
knowing the power of plow and pen,
the joy of harvest.

Mary L. Gardner

City Lights

Colors abound all over town
while subways snake beneath the ground.
Flashing lights find back-alley fights.
Yellow taxis weave and honk.
Buildings thick on every block.

Silver and gold trade on Wall Street.
Broadway beckons with summer heat.
People hurry from place to place.
Economy demands—pick up the pace.
Billboards announce. Pickpockets pounce.

It's the city,
      high fashion, slim rations,
            glamour and clamor.

Bobbie Dumas Panek

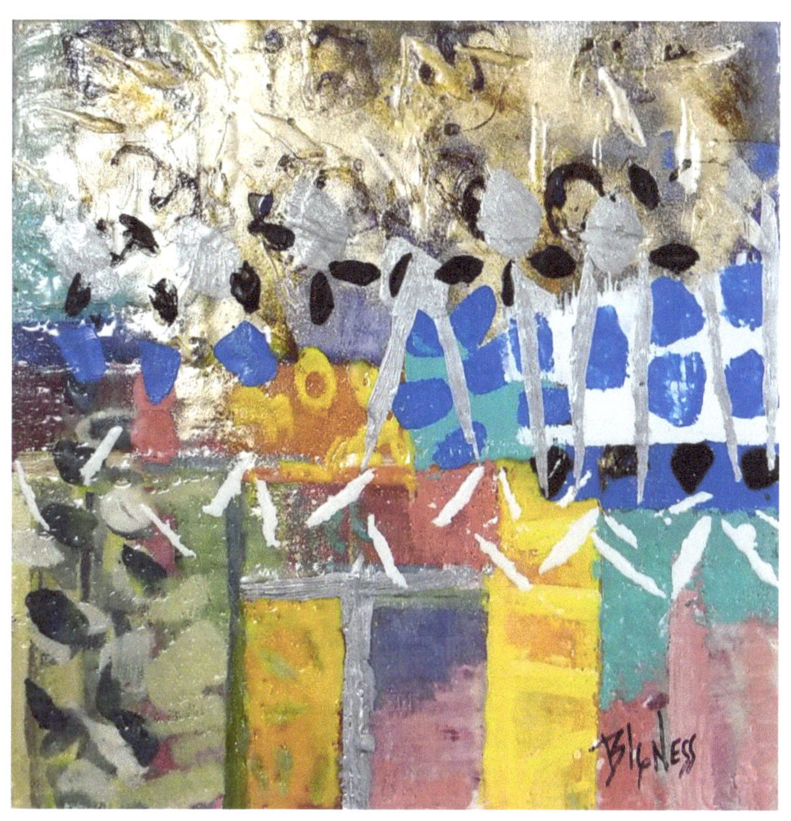

"City Lights" by Linda Bigness

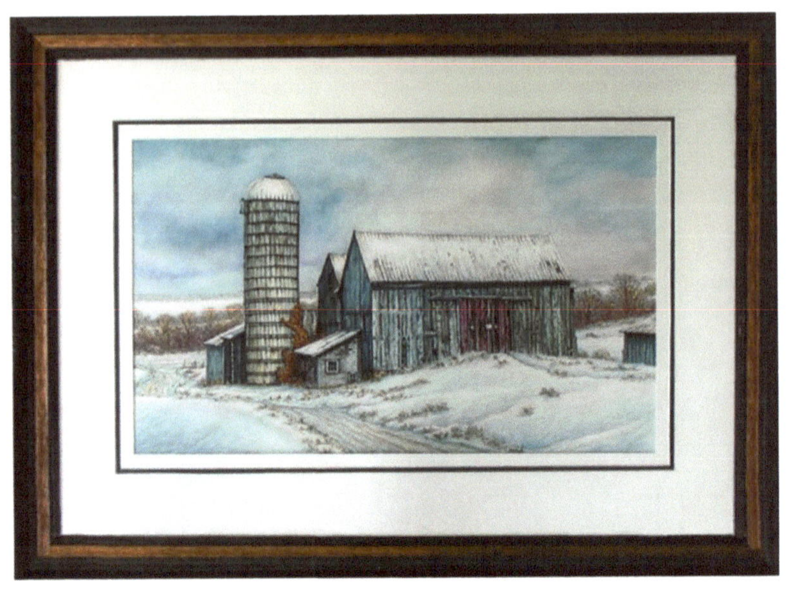

"Winter Barnscape" by Joan Stier

Winter Barnscape

Time was when sound of stanchions rattled with
movement of cows. Steam rose from nostrils of
Holsteins. Farmer Greg poured ground oats, corn,
soybeans, molasses, salt and minerals
from polyester/nylon feed bag onto piles
of corn silage in front of each cow.
They ate, flicked at pesky flies. Soft brown eyes
showed little interest in 92.1 crackling music
from transistor radio. Barn cats slinked in slanted
rays of sun. This building held promise with pregnant
heifers, full milk pails, bales stacked high in the mow.
Milking told time at 5 a.m. and 4 p.m. Farmyards
had clotheslines, wells with pumps, chickens
on the lawn. Now large operations with sprawling
buildings own thousands of head, milking-automated,
tags in ears determine how much feed is dispersed
to each cow. Pipelines carry milk, and music
is streamed by Sirius radio.

Bobbie Dumas Panek

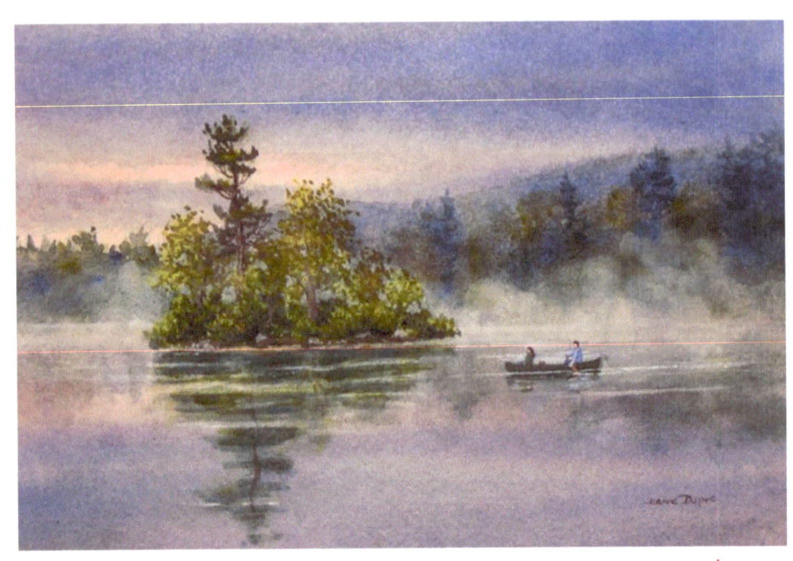

"Adirondack Sunset at Lake Lazurne"

by Jeanne Dupre

Adirondack Sunset

Canoes stream effortlessly along the calm water,
peaceful vision as the small island
seeks its boundaries
among the trees' reflection in the lake.

The sky sits silently above
in rose pink with midnight blue
horizontal washes
singing praises
of forests below.

Dreams are held
in secret pockets
of our heart
wishing for
continuity
and serenity.

Nancy Keats Benson

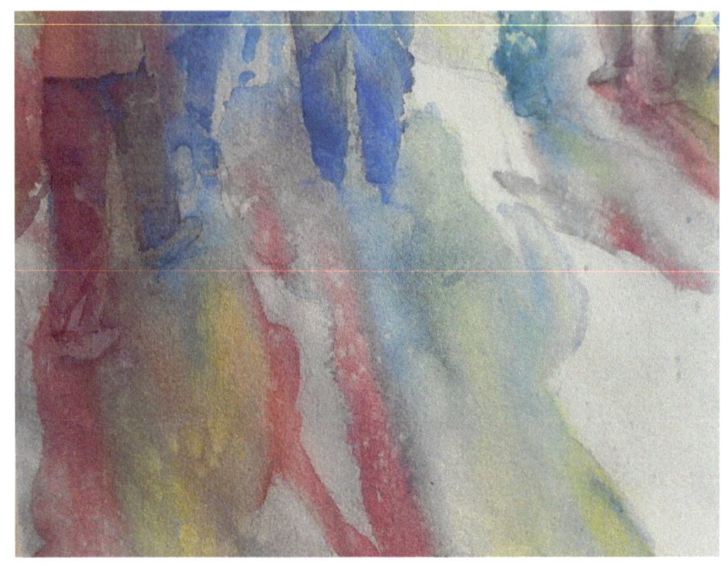

"Fire Drill" by Susan Murphy

Fire!

Feel the heat sizzle beneath your feet
like campfires of Union soldiers
while they talked inside Fort Sumter
just before rebels fired cannons
exploded this land into Civil War.

Founders of this great idea
knew it was imperfect, yet
generations of men and women
have sacrificed limbs, sight, lives
to defend the Constitution.

Pinocchio politicians,
add kindling to smoking fuel,
trade truth for power and lucre,
tie themselves in Gordian knots
to distort what happened January 6.

Do you hear alarm bells keening?
Like firemen, can we douse the flames
licking freedom's breached foundation
while spineless lawmakers kneel in fealty
to the one who lit this fire?

Judith McGinn

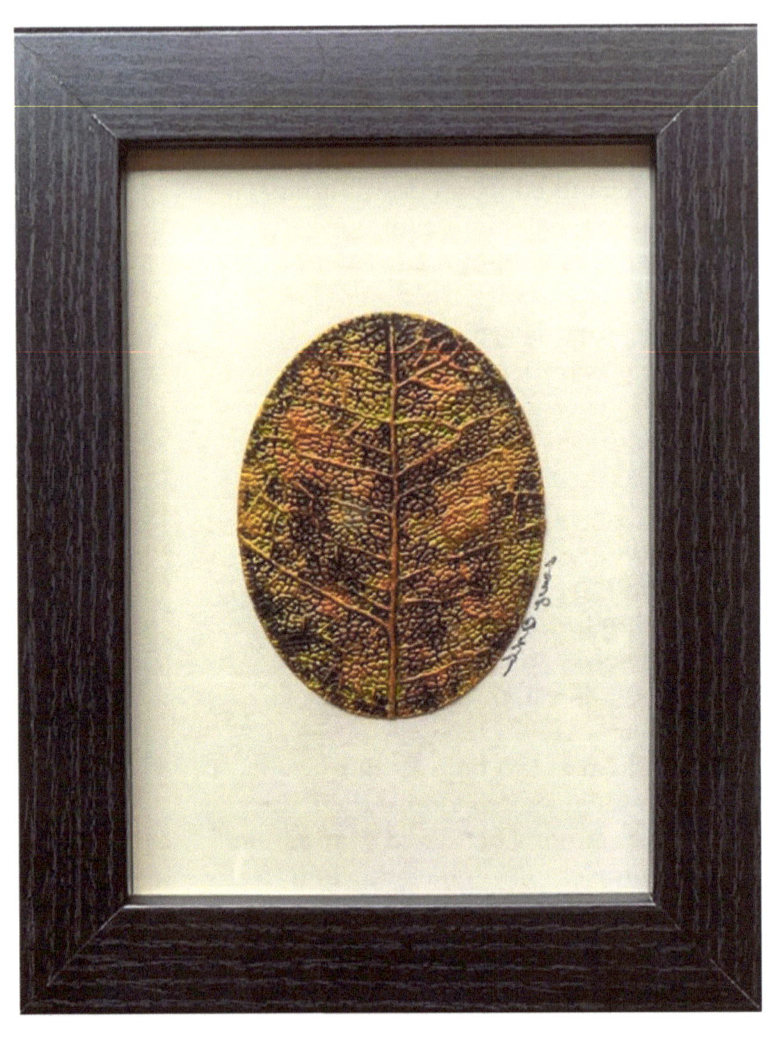

"Autumn Delight" by Sheila M. Byrnes

Summer Solstice

Solitary, gilded leaf reminds me
of fall's magic spell when leaves transform
landscape into a carnival of color
then return one-by-one to Mother Earth.
It moves me to savor this summer solstice,
light that lingers like memories of youth.

Today a sapphire sky wears a pearl
necklace of opalescent clouds.
Walking in my garden, I breathe in
fragrance of roses, brushes of lavender,
rushing to seed themselves in this brief season.
Autumn always comes so soon.

I stoop to pick astilbe flames and zinnias
for tonight's celebration, united again
with family, dear friends, illuminated
as last light slips below waving flora.
How can I think of autumn now
when I'm knee deep in flowers?

Judith McGinn

Lake Durant

Quiet, serene, rustic, private.
Motorboats outlawed; kayaks welcome.
Tents, illuminated by lanterns, raised by campers.
Hikers crunch on dried leaves and twigs through
winding pathways, pine scents intense.
Swimmers create eddies with their swirls.
Uninterrupted readers serenaded by songs
of mother birds.

Quiet fishermen hoping for bass or muskie dinners.
Children wonder at nature's kingdom.
Smoke of crackling campfires wend to the heavens
bringing aromas of wood-infused repasts.
Raccoons feasting on fish remnants
while campers slumber.

Karen Hempson

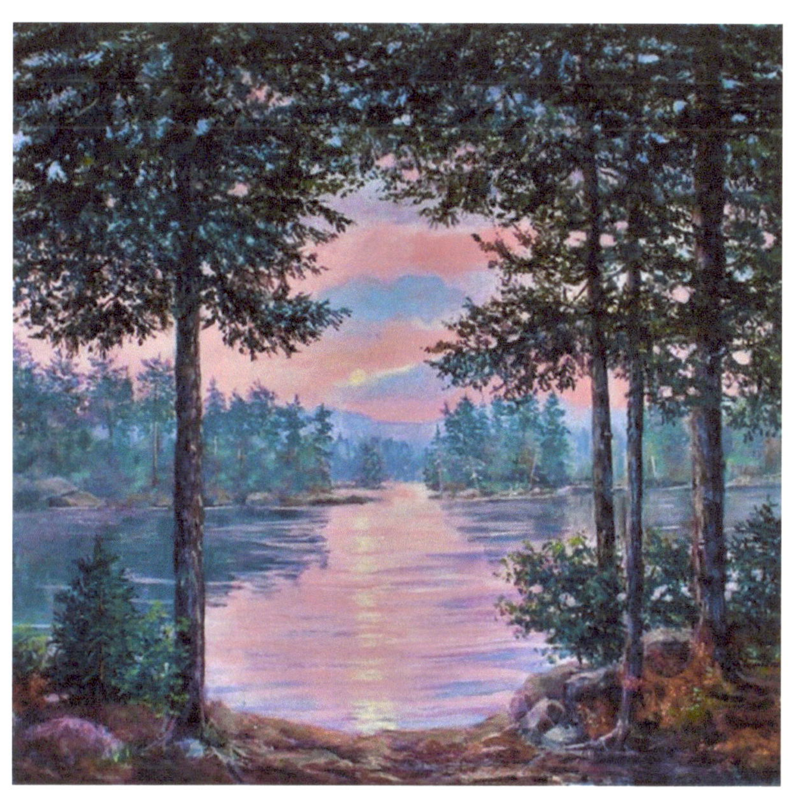

"Lake Durant Sunrise" by Jeanne Dupre

Art Speaks

Wait. Look again, listen. Bare your feet,
step softly in the sand,

stumble on the unexpected – shells, pebbles
and pendant, water-logged hairy chain of knots
torn from its tether, some tumult undefined.

Do I imagine more here than reason allows?
Do I employ fiction to convey some deeper truth?

Is it not true for artists, as it is for poets:
we receive and discover, assemble and disassemble,
begin and wait? Employ lines, tempos and rhythms,
color and shape, mysteries and tangibles of sound?

Is it not true that beneath our unresolved manufacture
lies the slow coming to light of what we mean to say,
by pen or palette?

Mary L. Gardner

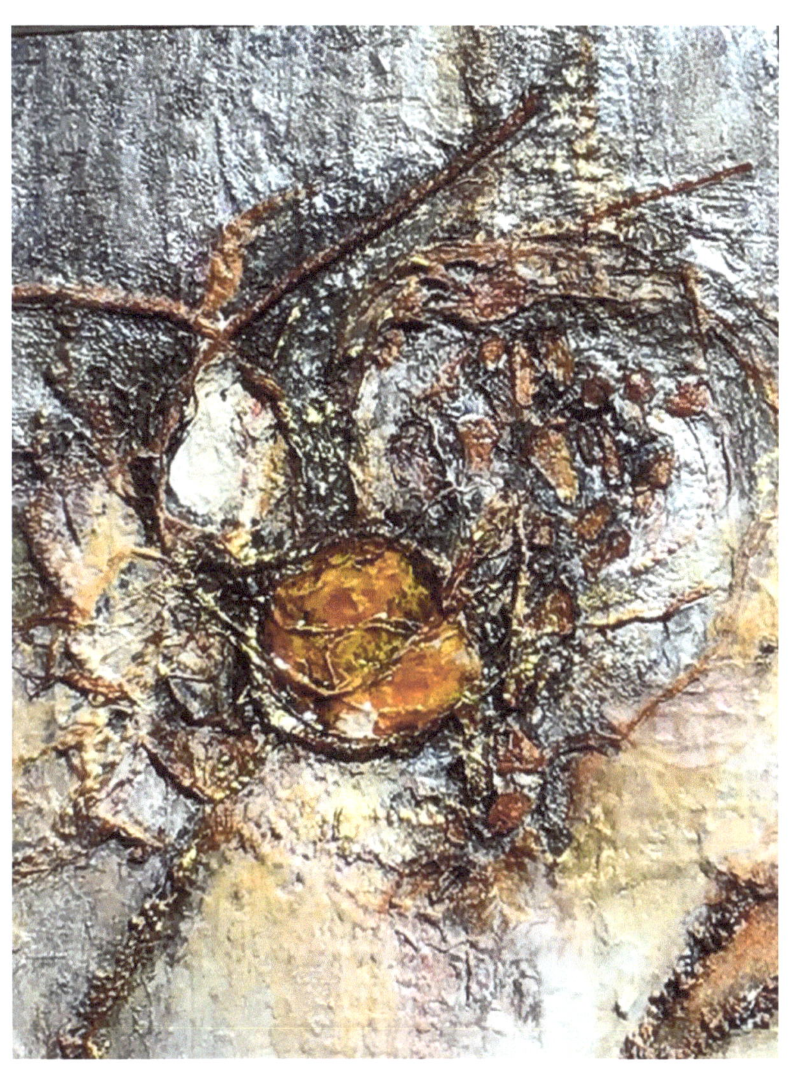

"Chaos" by Mary Raineri

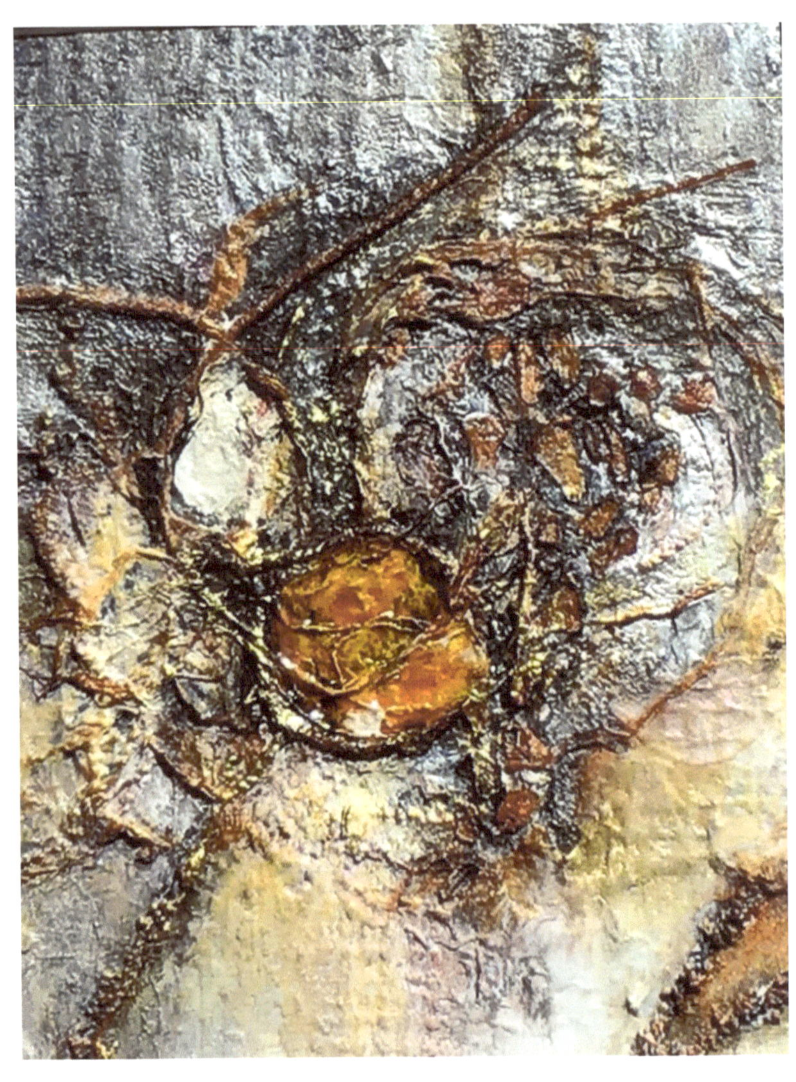

"Chaos" by Mary Raineri

Chaos

As if living under the knowledge of our deaths
weren't paradox enough, we misinterpret chaos
in an artist's brush strokes, color, texture, line;
each seemingly random marking seen as pattern.

Here decisions by the human artist inherent
for we are in love with arrangements, seeing a crowd
of human heads where colored blots are configured.
Raised and textured surface become landscape
imagined until it is, and shape of a woman in curves.
Lines where the sea withdrew from the desert.
Constellations drawn by a child's hand or a god's.

Within that apparent randomness, mathematical
repetitions: self-similarities, fractals that belie chance.
Non-linear configurations, interlinking templates
in which a man sees his face in the face of God
in an apple core. Symbols found in markings
leading to discoveries of similarities in images:
pictures of the human brain and the universe,
eye and nebula, birth of a cell and death of a star.

Golden Ratio and hierarchical structures:
perhaps not an angel on the head of a pin,
but then again, why not? Not all events have
overt cause, but structures have paradigms,
and paradigms have systemic order. Dichotomy
inherent in our cosmos in which, at any moment,
a hurling asteroid or comet streaks across wide,
dark sky at precisely the moment we look up,
searching for a missing son.

Nancy Avery Dafoe

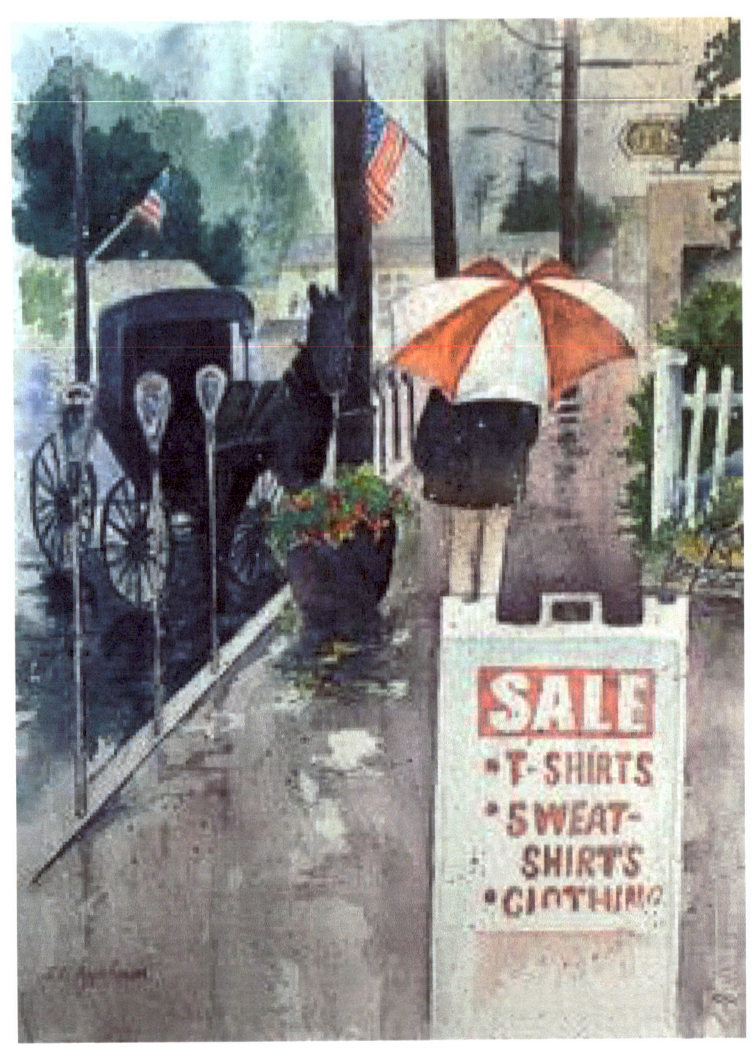

"Rainy Day, Alexandria Bay" by Joan Applebaum

Simple Encounters

Beside lush fields the Amish ride in
black buggies on the shoulders of roads,
"plain people" who are not really plain
once you look harder. Think more.
Builders roof in their hats and beards,
suspenders and simple blue shirts,
working hard, for the Bible tells them so.
At highway rest stops, they sell their wares:
pies, produce, honey.
The world passes more slowly with them,
and I wonder about simplicity.
Could I do it? Live without conveniences, electricity?
How often does this idea draw me? Call me?
Point out the uncluttered life of mind and heart?
On a village street a black horse harnessed
to a small black buggy waits patiently,
notices me. Stares. His eyes haunt me.
Around us, American flags hang on poles,
someone carries a large red and white umbrella.
Colorful blossoms nestled in their black planter
drink in the gentle rain.
I ponder ideas of minimalism and downsizing
my treasures, the beauty of color and blue skies,
art and poetry and books.
In a rush of contrasts, questions swirl
and I stare back at this horse.
Without technology, what would we miss?
Without progress, what would we lose?
Without thoughtfulness, acceptance of our differences,
what would we have?
Without all the noise, what is essential?
What price do we pay for our freedom to choose?

Janet Clare Fagal

Three Palm Trees

Sun's angle, sky blue draws
my eyes. Up. Three palm trees,
crowns round and fluffy as hens.
I chuckle. Shade my eyes, sigh.
Imagine I hear a bird cluck.

Four or five chickens, distant scatter
of barred, brown, red-crowned heads
bobbing. Claws scratch sand's edge,
nimble, prance away from waves.

You used to laugh at
hybrid chickens' fancy petticoats
when we went to the Fair. I lean
against a sun-warmed trunk,
feel earth's hum through it.

Busy beaks peck beach wrack
between palm roots.
Our heads bent, hands unspooling
long shadows.

Rachael Ikins

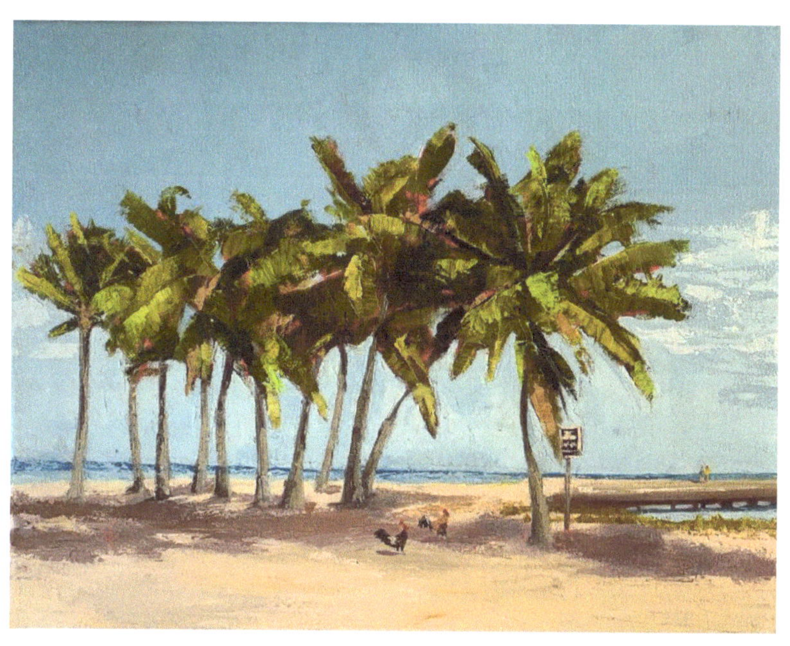

"Chicken of the Sea" by Patty Mabie

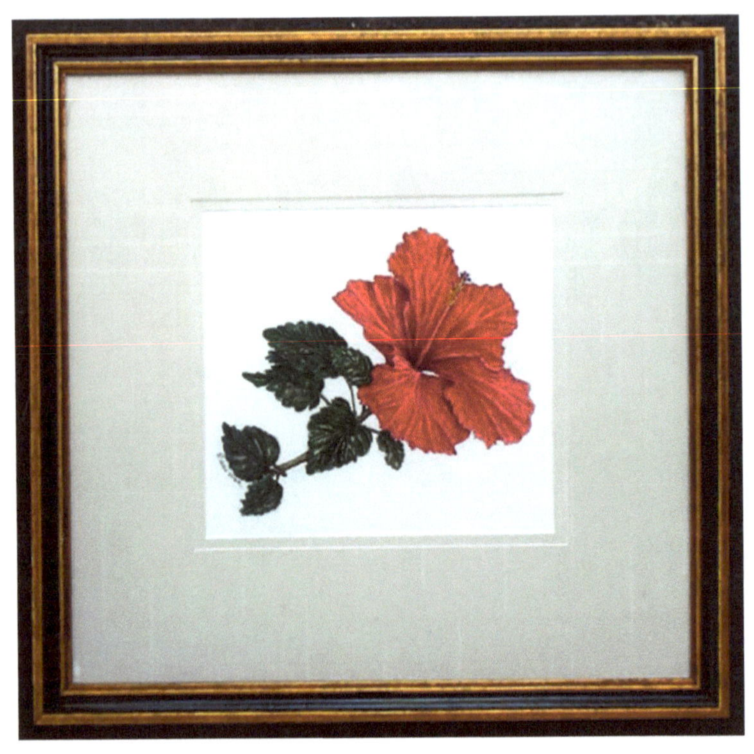

"Hibiscus" by Joan Stier

Ode to a Cactus Flower: Calling Me

Petals call my fingers,
mouth, stroke against
my cheek.
Cool silk alien.

Silence roars magenta
ecstasy, each dancer
swirls a wider skirt,
hides my face, those
taffeta folds.

Lavish.
Luscious.
Lipstick-slathered-on-glass, you
wester, melty
sunward.

My fingernail worries a splinter,
painful pleasure.
Trickling droplet, my blood's
color,

your velvet throat.
Swallow
me.

Rachael Ikins

II

Ekphrastic Responses to the "Made in New York" Exhibition at the Schweinfurth Art Center, 2021

Artists and "Made in New York" artwork in order of appearance

Knitting Lesson

Here, in the cool surround of brick and stone,
secluded space and slant of morning sun.

The lesson begins. Slow, quiet clicking
over and below, through hoops and pulls

of yarn and trust, hands and eyes bent on task,
life stories slipping in, disappearing

in the joy of process, not merely goal,
and the gift of time of one to the other.

Mary L. Gardner

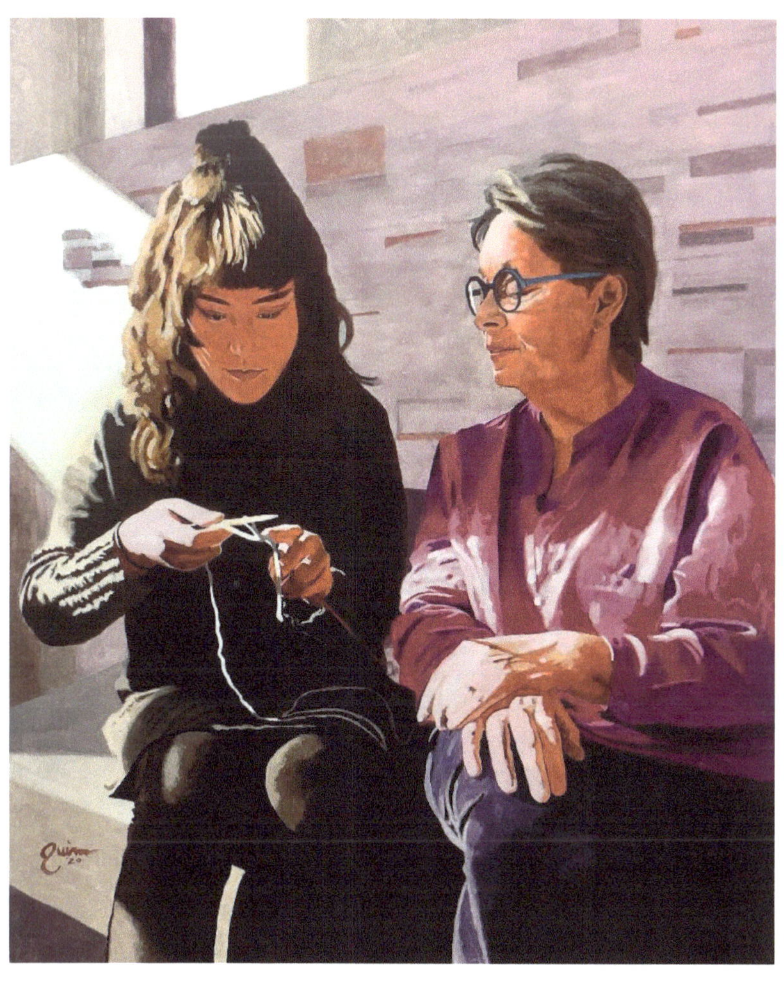

"Knitting Lesson, Portraits of Machangxum and Mary"

by Jim Quinn

Harriet Tubman

How do we honor the woman hiding beneath the icon that history has encased in concrete? How can we rescue her from a history that could hardly wait until Martin Luther King's body was in the ground to snatch his memory from J. Edgar Hoover's constant surveillance and eulogize him? To best honor King's memory, we must remember the U.S. government's successful attempt to demonize him to death and how hated he was in the country as he moved beyond Civil Rights to fight for economic justice. While we can certainly celebrate his "I Have a Dream" speech during Martin Luther King Day, let us also have students read his far more relevant and dangerous 1967 "Beyond Vietnam" speech, when, during the height of the war, King called the U.S. "The greatest purveyor of violence in the world today."

Similarly let us remember that Tubman lived in constant danger from Slavecatchers who tracked down and returned freedom takers to their unforgiving "owners" for the typical $100 reward; the 70 (low estimate) enslaved Maryland people she led to freedom worth about $7,000 to paid traffickers or almost $150,000 in today's purchasing power. She also collaborated with John Brown in planning the attempted slave revolt at Harpers Ferry in 1859. During the war, she multitasked as a spy, scout, and nurse for the Union, while planning and executing a military operation.

While the United States took the opportunity to honor King, opening the way for the story of a resolute American revolutionary to emerge, we now have a unique chance to appropriately honor Tubman, and bring her true story to our country's history.
(Continued)

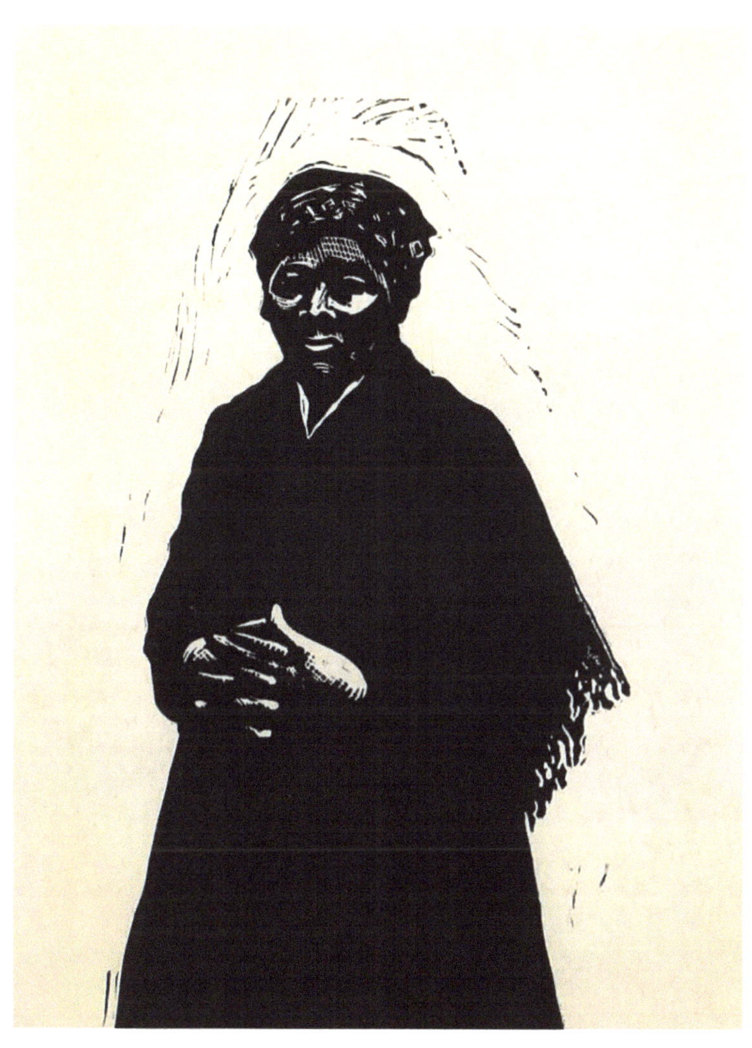

"Tubman" by Cyntia Cratsley

Harriet Tubman (*Cont.*)

The grassroots group, Women on 20s, held an online poll to choose a woman to recommend for the front of the $20 bill as the Treasury Department embarks on a major currency change. Tubman won the poll, which led to a monumental decision that must be made between the two possible options being considered. Should we choose a courageous patriot who risked her life and freedom to return repeatedly to assist at least 70 enslaved people to freedom on the Underground Railroad? Or should we go with a slave owner who offered bounty hunters $50 for the return of runaway human property, plus an additional $10 "for every hundred lashes" inflicted, and in addition forced Native Americans off their homelands?

Full disclosure: the fearless resister is Harriet Tubman, who served the Union during the Civil War. She would be the first woman's face on the currently all-male United States currency. The ruthless slave owner and instigator of the Trail of Tears is Andrew Jackson, seventh President of the United States, who is currently on the bill. If you value truth in history, take action, in the spirit of King and Tubman. Write your Congressional representatives and the Treasury Department today and demand that Tubman replace Jackson, who has no place worthy of honor on United States currency.

Dr. Sally Roesch Wagner

Her Red Cloak

She was up all night after a lumbar puncture
with chemo, then ended up needing
blood transfusion, but by the time
her nausea began to fade,
it was the middle of the night,
when a nurse brought her snacks and drink.
Thank you, thank you, she thought she said.

Someone gave her a red blanket to warm her
as she took a few tentative steps
in the right direction.
Still uncomfortable and in pain,
she does not wince or cry, bravely imagining
her flaming red blanket as the cloak
of a dancer flying across the stage
or as mantle of an ailing superhero avenger
because she will beat this unseen enemy
with a little help.

Someone told her, the color red helps stimulate
appetite and alleviate depression, but all she
knows for certain is that she feels stronger
wearing it, less anxious.

In that interstitial hallway between illness
and health, she is of two minds,
almost two physical bodies,
and she sees one turning away
and one moving forward.

Even though she knows a bone marrow
biopsy awaits, she works to suppress the dread,
but a headache causes her to make her way back
to her hospital bed where a young man is waiting
(Continued)

Her Red Cloak *(Cont.)*

not with flowers or silly comments
but an anxious yet hopeful face, his hand reaching
out as she crosses that threshold.

"From illness to health," he says with a slight smile.
"What?" she asks, momentarily confused.
"That's where you are dancing off to," he says,
helping her to the bedside.
"Oh, how did you?"
"I saw you dancing in the hall."
"How could you? I only moved a few steps."
"Ah, but they were dancer's steps."

"It's my red cloak," she says, lifting the red blanket
with one, unsteady hand,
letting it fly.

Nancy Avery Dafoe

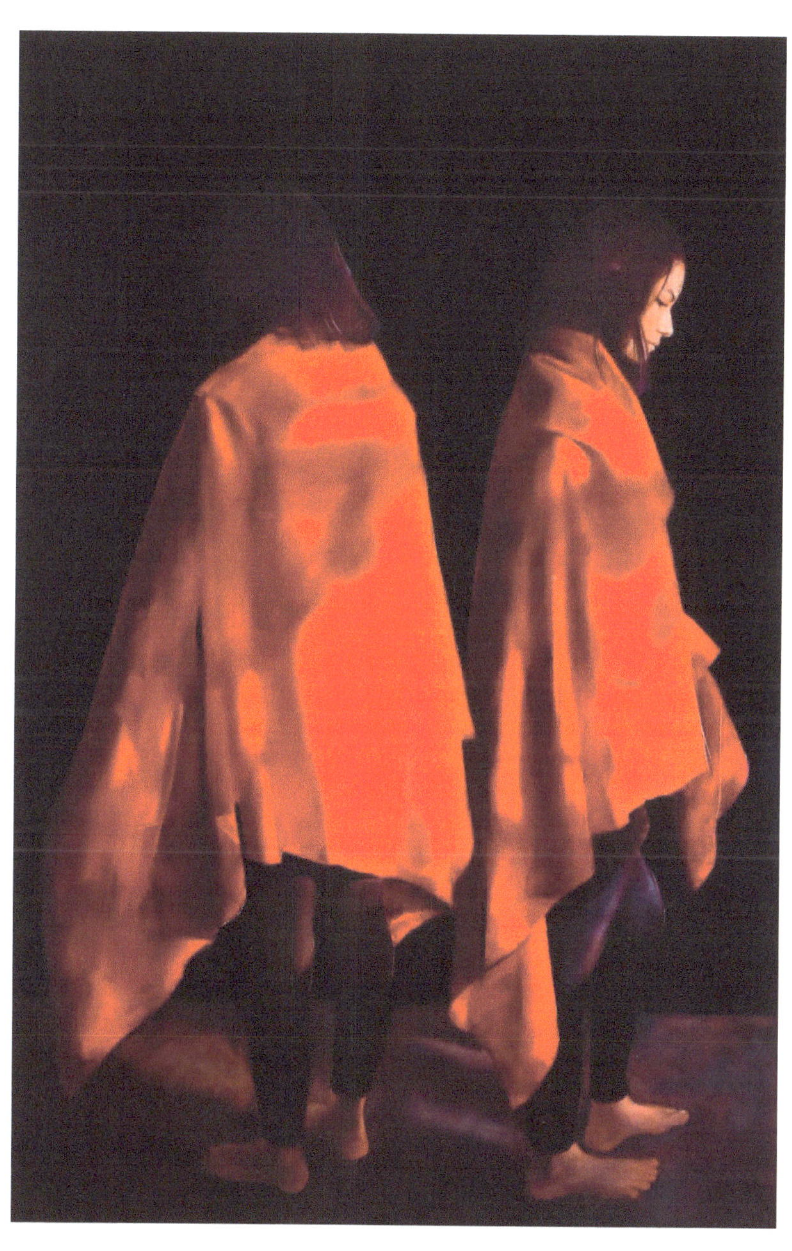

"Duo" by John Fitzsimmons

Here

From ships' holds, bodies jumbled together.
Tribes, languages, mixed in a sea of dehydration,
diarrhea, terror, ever present whip lash.

Dumped here in cages and lots, auctioned off, beaten,
raped. Worked to death in cotton and cane fields,
pregnancy no excuse to stop. So many attempts
to escape, into swamps, chased by dogs.

Caught, hung, trussed and flogged on an immaculate
lawn while petticoated white women and men
barbecued pork ribs. Ate at a linen-draped table,
close enough you could smell the food.

As your flesh stripped, divots dropped, snatched by dogs.
Your manhood cut away and still white children played.
Adults sipped juleps. You ignited: flames took your
voice, your people ordered to stand. Here.

Then the war, the signature that said, "Free"
one June 19th. Fleeing north. Jumbled in cities,
untrained in anything but field work, struggle to adapt
to freedom. Here, to more spit on your cheeks.
You raised white children, worked their railroads.
Bathrooms, bus seats, schools "your own."
Not equal. Here.

They cut down the woods behind your old house
and left a naked field. No houses, no life except
that of tiny feet living their lives below
the surface. Grasses and wild flowers spread roots,
adapted to hardship. To men with chainsaws,
heavy machinery.
(*Continued*)

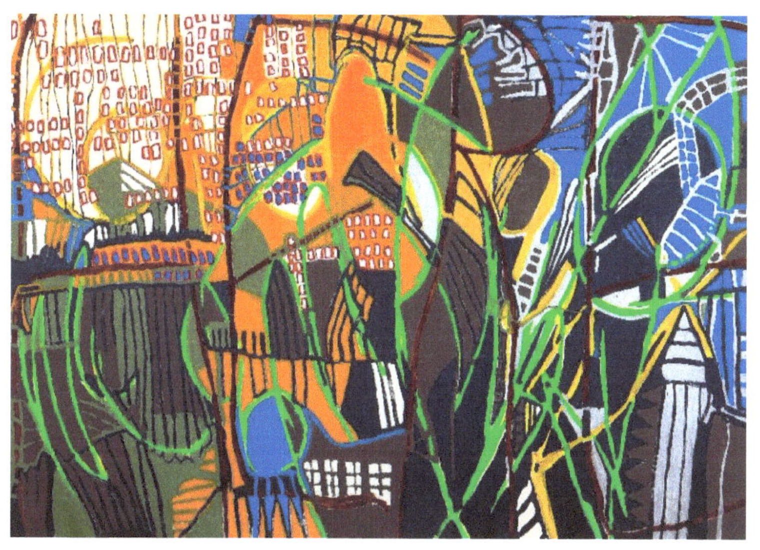

"Here" by Carole Inverno

Here (*Cont.*)

"SOLD." Asphalt buried trillium, bloodroot, goldenrod.
Self-storage units appeared and with them,
sedge grasses and other plants too stubborn to die,
cracking the pavement to reach sunlight, to drink rain.
Here. Jumbled by bulldozer blade, staying alive.

As you stay alive.
Trudging through storms
of bigotry.
Bandaged wounds, found a seat
on a bus, a counter stool at a diner.
Work three jobs to feed your kids,
make do and make do and make do until
you sent your eldest to college.
First university student in the family.

You never forget that weight, tar-burning skin.
June 19, 2021 after a year of too many more black men
and women murdered, white police begin to be held
accountable.

Your clouds of kinky hair,
your woven nest of bundled braids,
skin mahogany to lightest cream,
sensuous colors, with music that speaks to the heart
in ways no Beatle or Rolling Stone ever will,
Aretha insisted. Respect.
You say, "I am here.
I am everywhere."

Rachael Ikins

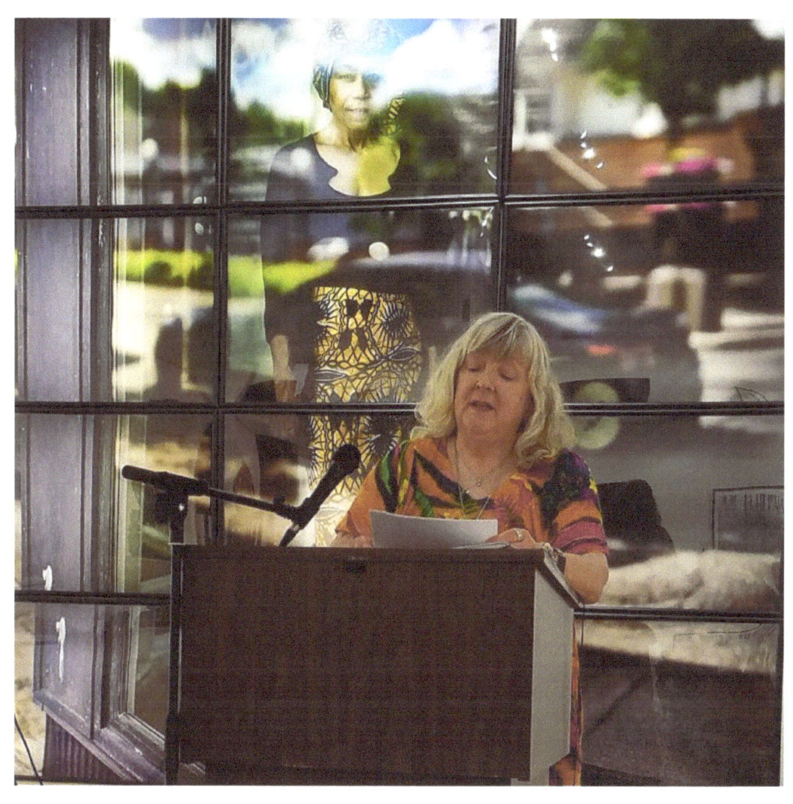

Rachael Ikins reading at the Schweinfurth Art Center

Photo by Janet Fagal

Untitled

Hands three join
Black White Brown
Arch over one woman
Clothed in green
Earth's desire
Spirit light matter
Earth wind fire
Look, she says,
Read the rainbow
Cloak of many colors
Mantle of the world
New young faces
Gather at the table
All our future there

Maureen McCarthy

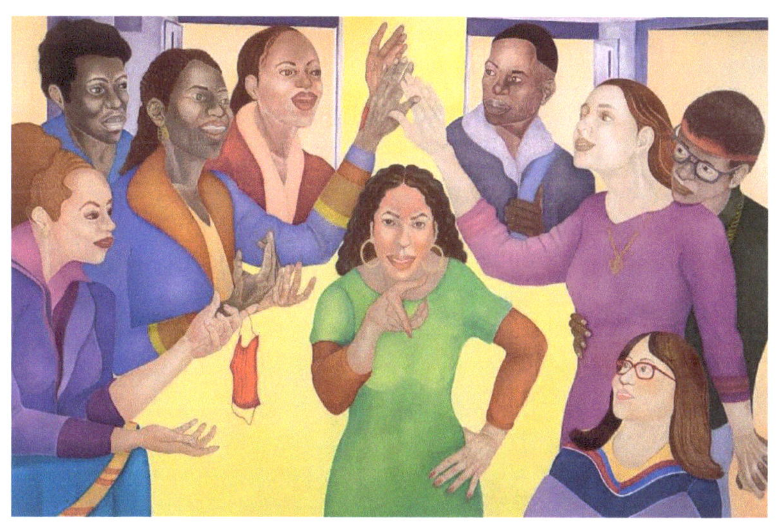

"School Lunch, 20" by Lisa Deloria-Weinblatt

Uncertainty

As in other world mythologies, bizarre only
because we are so programed to recognize location
but now displaced. Shakespeare's plays imbued
with uncertainty, as we recall experiencing this
most unsettling state approaching Glasser's
"Holding Patterns, #7," even texture of oil on linen
canvas causing hesitancy. Ambiguity dominates
with lines between offerings of sky and skyline
before upended, position and place considered
as cityscape and displaced worlds. Space between
East River and Brooklyn or Hudson and Manhattan
only imagination here in this voluminous locus
in art center and the work of art.

No more than rectangle of blue with browns
below, and hints of buildings through partial
markings—the mind's eye takes them all the way
to windows. Grays and blues of deepening shades
are manifest, and then there are, suddenly appearing,
black post impressions also suggestive but of what?
Black floating signifiers become abandoned pier.

Even in abstractions, we imagine what is subtly
suggested. We fill in spaces with images known
in their water-based transference of medium
to fluidity, altering realism: a work the writer
will view and people in this "other world"
in which walking is outlawed and transport
achieved through visualization. Alternate region
technological yet primitive, with black warning
markers overhead, spires not of churches
but needle-like points of incision into the body
of the surreal, recognizable as our uncertainty.

Nancy Avery Dafoe

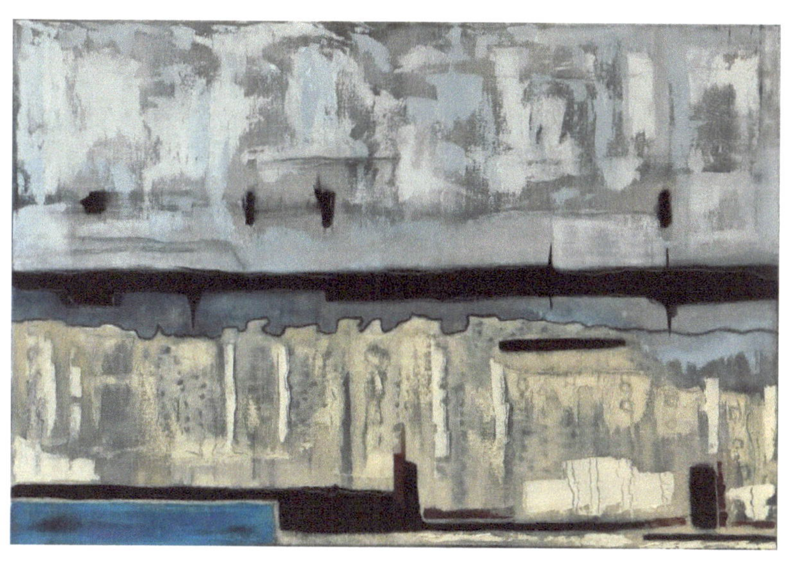

"Holding Patterns, #7" by Cora Jane Glasser

Alone, 2021

The alarms sound.
"Quiet now…," the teacher says,
"Hurry! Duck and cover."
I am ten. Somehow, I know
this desk, these walls,
will not save us
from a nuclear bomb.
Or radiation sickness.
I imagine myself after:
frightened, hungry.
Alone.

What if my family died, if everyone was gone?
Would I want to survive?
In my dreams I watch a girl in a train car.
No one else in sight. The train on an endless
loop travels from station to station.
Every seat, save hers, empty.
I am glad when the coldness of this nightmare
finally ends.

It is 2020. I am old. The new millennium
arrived in style with great hope and fanfare;
at least for a while, I was hopeful
that better days were ahead.
But then, 9/11.
Now we are in lockdown worldwide.
Afraid, worried, incredulous.
The enemy? A virus.
Invisible, tiny, unknown.
Deadly.
Called the *novel coronavirus,*
a name that seems oxymoronic to me.
I love books, especially poetry and novels,
(*Continued*)

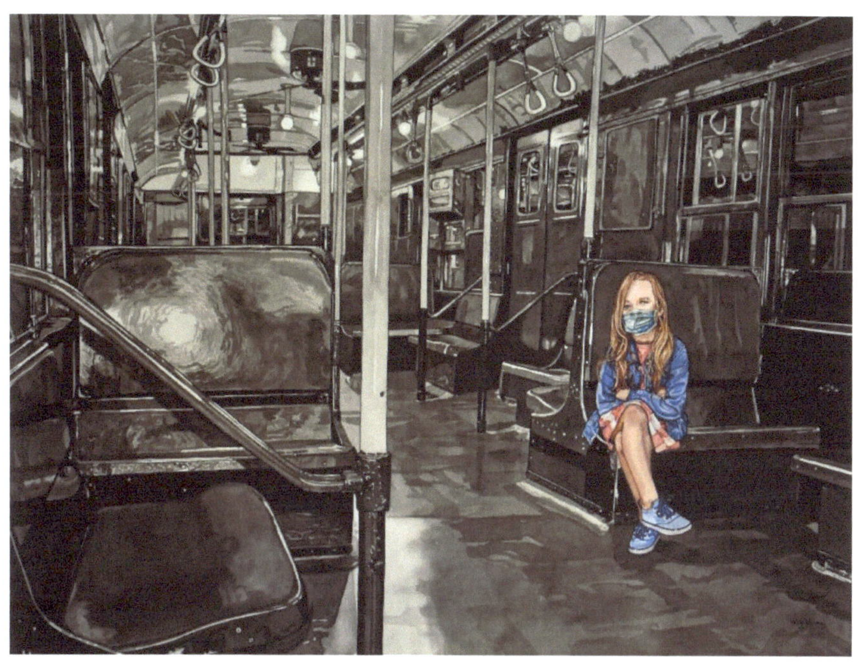

"Here, But Now They're Gone" by Valerie Patterson

Alone, 2021 (*Cont.*)

and new things intrigue,
even enjoy a Corona beer
every now and then.
At first this almost seems a silly name,
but this virus is no joke.
It's a pandemic.
Millions die alone in hospitals,
nurses' cell phones and iPads the only link to
panicked family, the only way to say goodbye.
My cousin dies from the virus.
Alone.
Others I know lose loved ones, still others suffer
from lasting effects.

When we finally emerge from our cocoons
masked, sanitized and blessedly vaccinated,
I feel tentative, off-kilter, unsure.
I am in need of art more than food.
Friends, more than books.
And hope more than anything.
In a gallery in 2021, I see a painting of a girl on a train.
The mask she wears is illusory. It keeps her
from spreading germs,
but it will not protect her. She sits on this train.
Alone.
Tiny and scared.
I am pulled back in time. Has this painter
dreamed my dream?
I shake my head. There are too many questions.
Where, I wonder, is hope?

Janet Clare Fagal

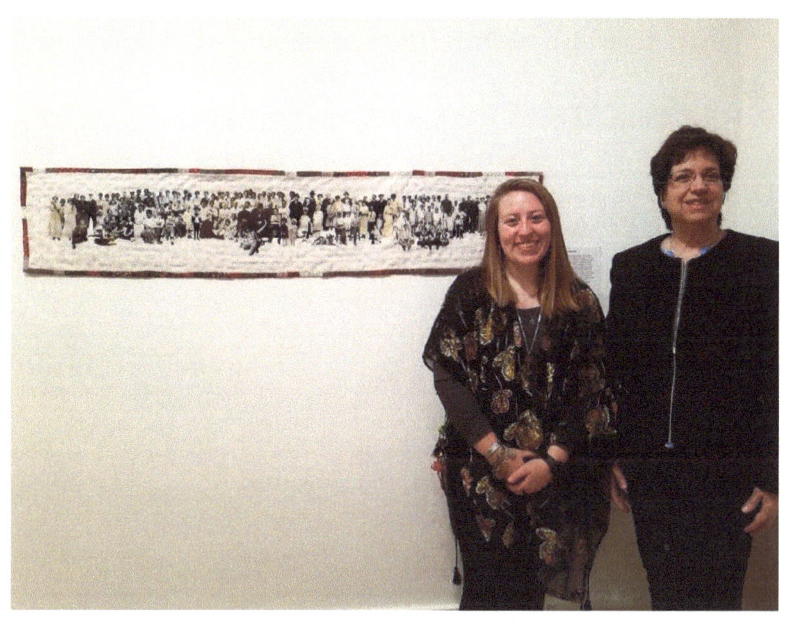

Pen Woman Janet Clare Fagal with artist
Allison Piedmonte at the Schweinfurth Art Center.
Photo by Judith McGinn

Two Ladderback Chairs

Two ladderback chairs on deep inky canvas,
the eye tracking similarity and symmetry
without consciously acknowledging principles
behind Carlson's design in which emphasis
on the simplicity of two chairs is of equal weight,
but the movement and patterns created
by linen cloth instructs in variety
while reinforcing repetition
and contrast in the topography.

So aligned was William Carlos Williams'
red wheelbarrow beside the white chickens,
a poem in which simplicity held nothing
less than the secrets of creating art.

Balance, emphasis, pattern, unity, proportion,
and hierarchy established. White linen
suggesting sacraments: a chalice veil,
an altar cloth in various positions, asymmetrical
yet of equal weight on their deliberately
off-centered line; white for purifying
in liturgical practice, yet the pop
of contrast against rich blue-black frame
belies hierarchy, smaller elements lighter
yet with greater import.
Chairs empty.

Color psychology at work in Carlson's
background of mimetic desire,
suggesting stability, calming presence,
reliability, and strength to offset
muted yellow of the pine chairs
and fine white linen,
(Continued)

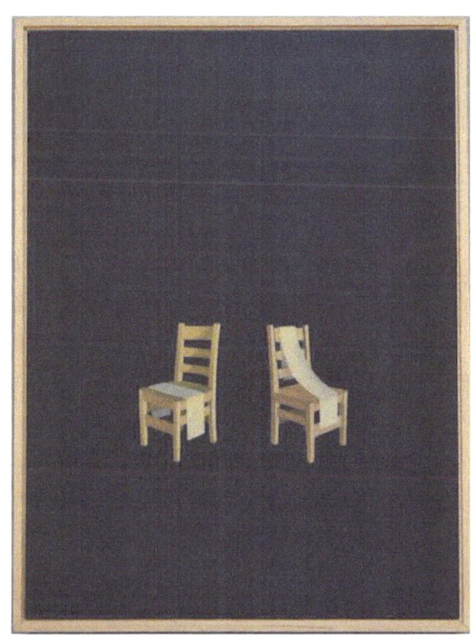

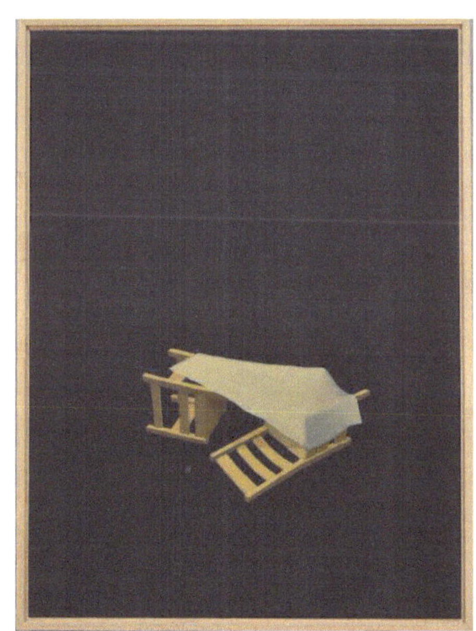

"Untitled I and II" by Stephen Carlson

Ladderback Chairs (*Cont.*)

this painting perfection in aesthetic
and design principles, subtly referencing
Van Gogh's two paintings of chairs,
one of "somber wood" and the second,
Gaugin's counter balance; empty chairs
symbolic of mortality and the tension between.

Only if Carlson's "Untitled" two chairs is viewed
beside his next in the sequence will viewers notice
the juxtaposition of ladderback chairs upended,
liturgical cloths astray in the second, Gestalt
principles at work in both, yet quietly subverted.

Secrets of the artist right in front of you.

Nancy Avery Dafoe

freedom's promise

a space provided
walking with the fresh grass
wafting through the air
inner depth of colors,
muted pinks and blues,
sensing each brush stroke
facing all surfaces
with renewed strength
to see sunlight and hope
in future skies.

Nancy Keats Benson

Inspired by Robin Arnold's "Ocean Heat"

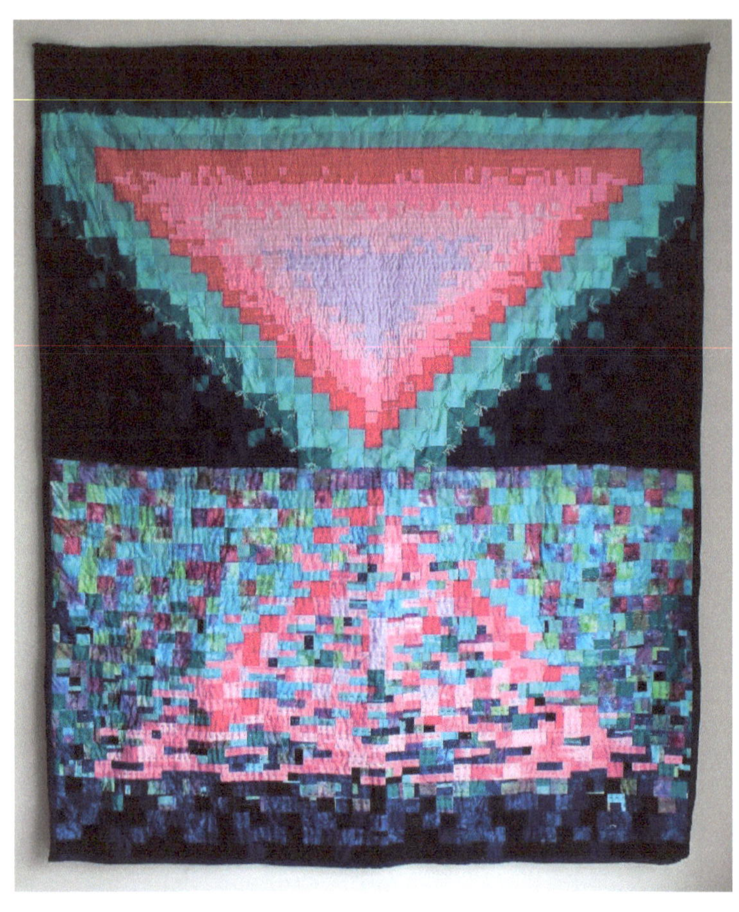

"88 Years Adrift" by Kevin Carr

Lifelines

When we lived on the farm
my mother hosted a circle
of friends for a quilting bee.
Fabric was stretched on a frame,
four sides blocked by sets of legs.
Libby and I played underneath,
tried to guess which shoes
belonged to which woman.
Sometimes I tickled Mother's toes,
giggling when she jiggled away.
Unlike Kevin Carr's abstract quilt,
mother used classic patterns,
double wedding ring, log cabin,
flower basket, to keep us
warm in winter, squares cut
from clothes damaged or outgrown:
last year's short sets, jumpers, blouses,
the sailor dress I wore to Sunday school.
I fondly remembered each one.
As I grew, she taught me to sew.
The last project we made together
was a summer star with saved scraps
of clothing worn by family now gone.

Happy memories bound me
to Eighty-eight Years Adrift.
An inverted sail, tied to rigging
with sailor hitch knots, fixed
against blue-black horizon,
hints of lone star and night sky.
Patterns reflected on a shimmering sea,
suggest sunrise or sunset.
Pieces of color float away,
(Continued)

Lifelines *(Cont.)*

mingle and merge, some returning
with black clinging like barnacles.
Random imperfections deliberate,
I imagine the artist's disconnection,
emotions of loneliness, grief.
Time falls overboard, drowns.
Night after night, he sleeps
rocked by waves of hope, despair.
Stitches blend, or contradict patches,
sometimes disappear altogether.
By patience, endurance, acceptance,
a journey into inner depths, an artist,
saved by his own lifelines.

Judith McGinn

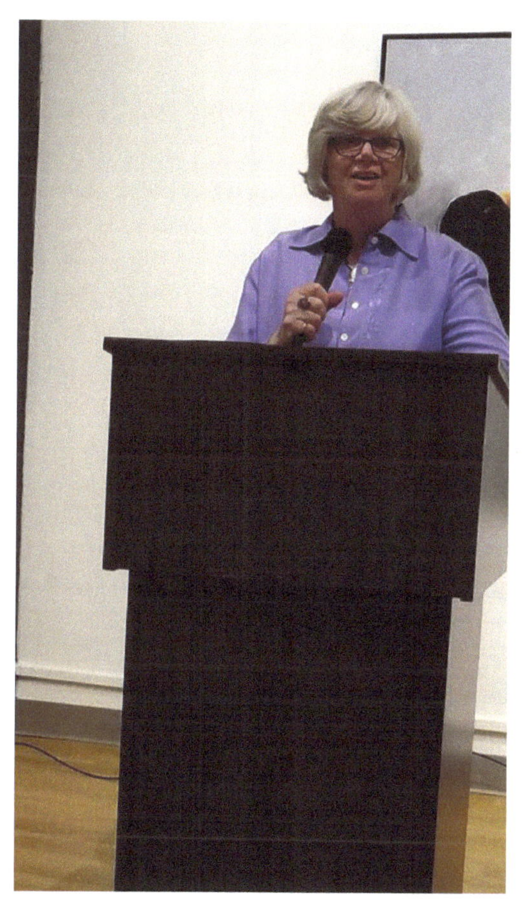

Judith McGinn reading at the Schweinfurth Art Center.

Photo by Janet Fagal

In Yellow Houses

Mothers taught daughters as they were taught.
Plant flowers. Tend gardens. Be polite. Obey elders.
Don't climb trees, run wild, or speak every thought
that comes into your mind.

Some imagined different futures for their girls.
Fathers and boys worked outside in fields, offices,
government, trades, tramped home ravenous and tired.
Their bulk, reeking sun-sweat usurped sweet-baked
kitchen air. Harried girls set tables, cleared and washed
dishes, unaware of roles imposed, like unfiltered sun
tunneling deep into skin and psyche. Girls grew
accustomed to staring out windows while sweeping,
mopping. Stitched dreams and ambitions into quilts,
aprons, ruffled dresses and shirtwaists.

Some joyfully embraced home as their domain.
Others felt trapped like Angelou's caged birds.
Shadows of girls in wall papered rooms, like Gilman's
damaged Mary, generations, vanished into mists of time.

In each generation, a courageous few broke out,
spoke up, until legions of women united, rallied,
marched, gained suffrage, demanded equal rights.

Glass domes continue to break. Still, late at night,
inside decayed, yellow houses, one can hear weeping
from soul-weary women.

Judith McGinn

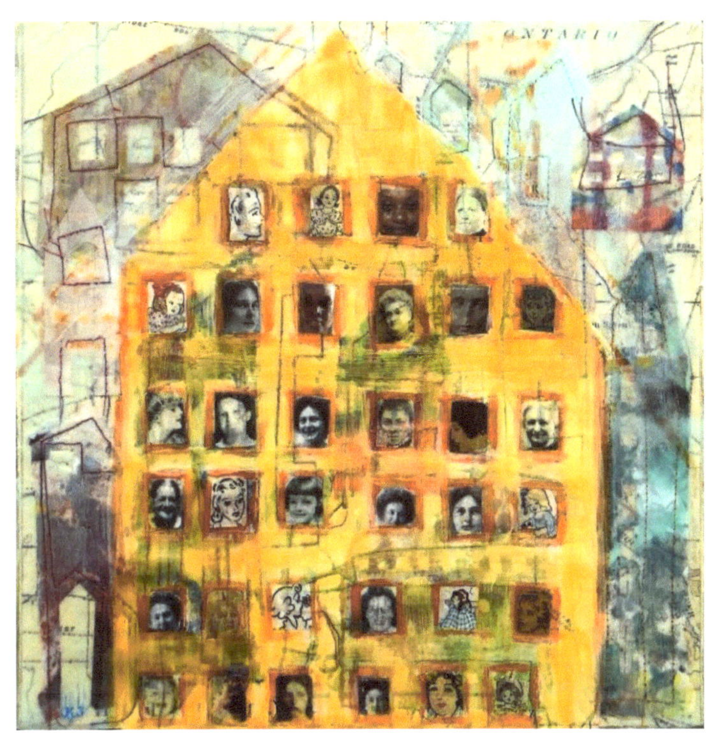

"Girls in the House" by Jean K. Stephens

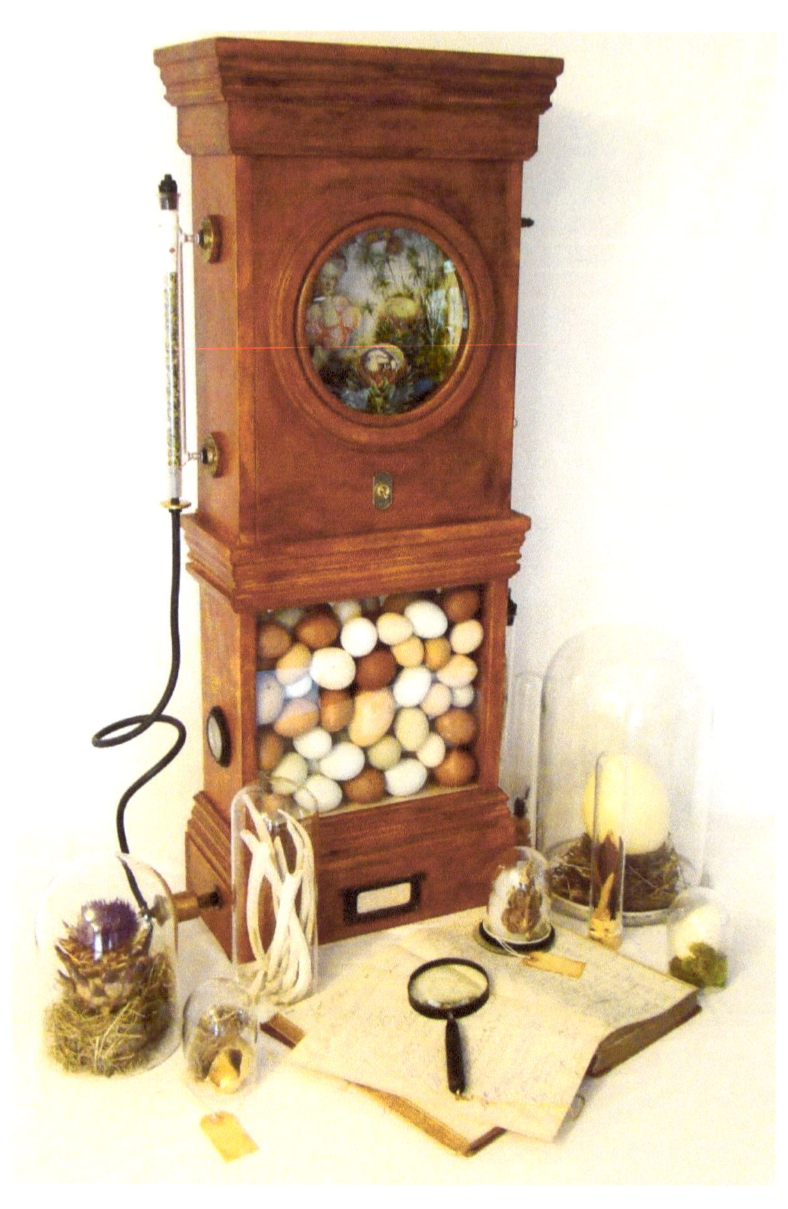

"Specimen No. 784" by Nancy Callahan

74

Dream Collectors

A ship glides up the Amazon River, onboard a man,
a colleague of Darwin, hungry for knowledge, fame,
a collector of rare birds, nests with eggs, an oologist.

Feathers, nests, a bird skeleton, clock case with
mass of eggs in varying sizes and colors, specimens
in space where time conveyed its passing to the living;
as seen through a porthole, a creature half bird/half
woman protects her egg, ready to hatch a human child,
an artist's reimagining of a naturalist's dream.

In my youth, mornings my sister and I slipped on
rubber boots, pulled baskets from the pantry, swished
through dew to the henhouse, ground splotched
like a Pollock painting. Two rows of hens dozed
on nests of hay. A jewel thief, I slid my hand under
warm bellies, fingertips searching for eggs. To me,
they were a breakfast staple, ingredient for desserts.

While climbing a tree, I found a nest with tiny, blue
eggs. My sister said they would turn into baby robins.
My mind veered from robins to chickens. "Will hen
eggs we collect be baby chicks?" The idea flooded me
with disgust and guilt. She whispered, "Don't worry.
Only rooster's girlfriends have baby chicks."

When I fell in love with my mate, new life waited within
my own eggs. I dreamed they'd grow into kind humans.
All creatures dream their young will thrive in the world.

As I sit at my desk and begin to write, I select each word,
dream of an embryo evolving into a fully-fledged poem
winging its way to another dreamer.

Judith McGinn

Musical notes pull from black fabric

fill room with sound
sharps and flats
pitch perfect
swirl into spaces
seeking song
history relies on
familiar chants
Gregorian and other
metal drums
hollow coconuts
flutes, didgeridoos
stream through woods
between mountains
heard below decks
on sailing ships
bulge from bugles
quiver taut strings
resonate to
remember

Bobbie Dumas Panek

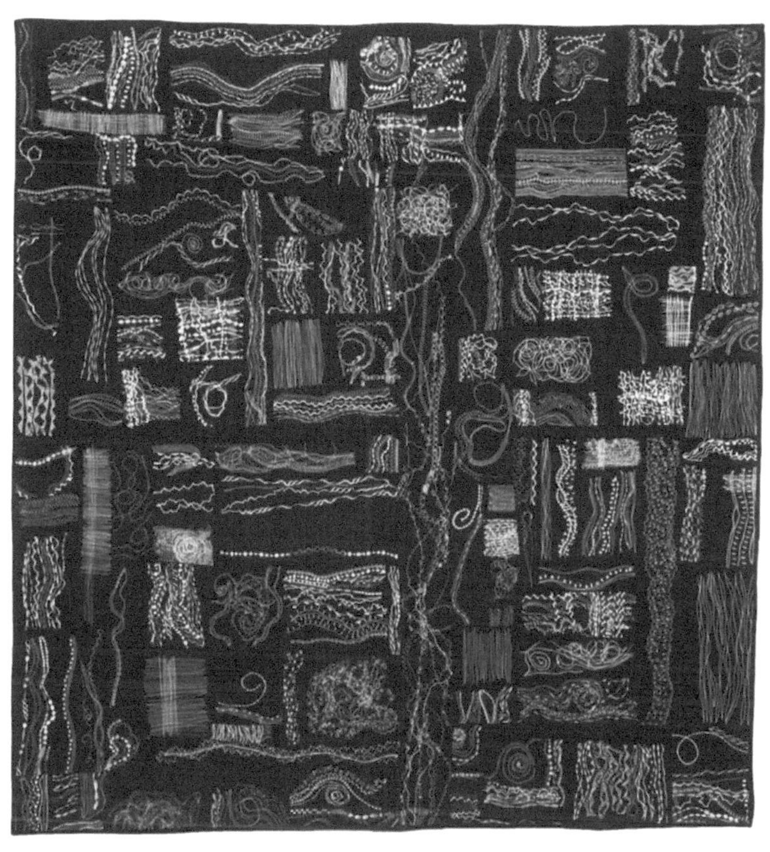

"Drawing II" by Susan Byrnes

Doll

She sees herself for the first time
as he sees her, nothing more than mannequin
missing an arm. Flawed, to be discarded.

Stuffed fabric of tightly woven cotton exposed
beneath her smooth, softly pink layer of plastic.
A murderous dark line between her neck
and the base of her head is expanding.
Her satin party dress torn and dirtied,
and its seams are not what they seemed.
Even her bright red hair of bouncing curls
was never her own.

Her face turns away to that flat, black
plain of existence in which her resolve
slowly tightens until, like the metal coils
within, she springs back,
picking up her limb and her chin
before walking out of his scene
to create one of her own.

Nancy Avery Dafoe

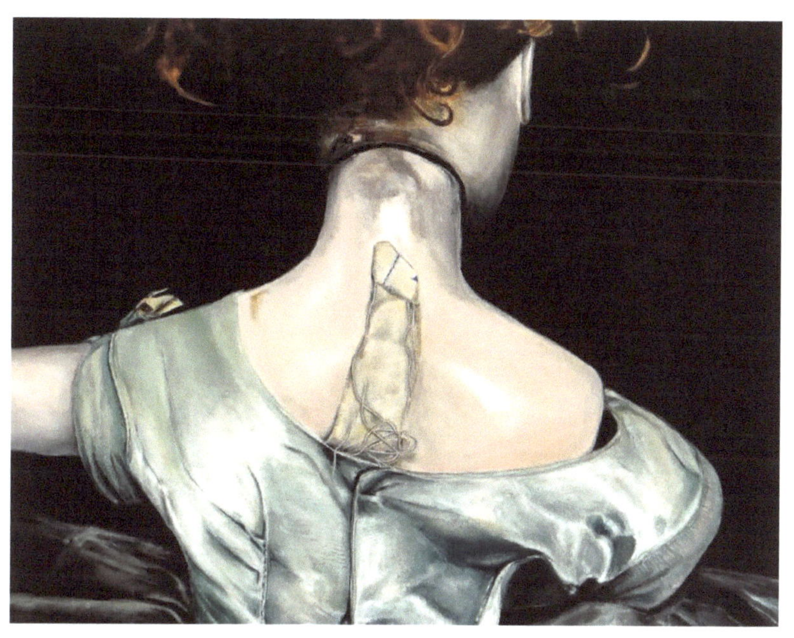

"Tangle" by Barbara Hart

Pen Women Contributors

Art Speaks, The Catalogue
An Anthology of Artwork and Ekphrastic Writing
Commemorating the 95th Anniversary
of the CNY Branch of the NLAPW

Contributors/CNY Branch Members

(A) Joan Applebaum is a visual artist and instructor who has taught in a variety of art centers throughout Upstate New York and Coastal Delaware. She holds memberships in two branches of the NLAPW-- CNY and Holly Branches. Her colorful paintings of the woodlands and waterways of Upstate NY, Thousand Islands Region, and Coastal Delaware are in private collections across the US and abroad. Visit www.windyhillstudioarts.com to see samples of Joan's artwork.

(L) Nancy Keats Benson is a retired Speech-Language Pathologist. She has been writing since high school when she had a wonderful creative writing course with Miss Nelson. She has two poetry books and a children's mystery book published. She's had many poems published in magazines and anthologies. Recently she had a nature poem published in an anthology, *Love Letters to Gaia*.

(A) Linda Bigness-Lanigan holds a BFA from Syracuse University and a MA in art history from SUNY Empire. Her work has been collected and exhibited throughout the United States. The most recent acquisition is a large-scale oil painting reflecting urban renewal, where it was placed in the Rochester, New York Regional Health Center.

(A)(L) Sheila M. Byrnes is a respected genealogist, freelance writer, and mixed-media artist. She has been published in several national magazines and currently writes the *CNYGS E-News,* a national bi-weekly genealogy newsletter. Her work is included in *Hopeful, Grateful, Strong,* an anthology of cancer survivors in Onondaga County, and *In the Company of Women.* Byrnes serves as the NLAPW National First Vice President and as the National Historian.

(L) Nancy Avery Dafoe writes fiction, nonfiction, and poetry and
has eleven books through independent publishers. Her novella
Naimah and Ajmal and a memoir about her son, *Unstuck in Time, A
Memoir and Mystery on Loss and Love* were released in 2021. She
previously wrote the memoir *An Iceberg in Paradise: A Passage through
Alzheimer's*. In addition to her three Goodwin mystery novels, Dafoe
has two published poetry books. She has also written books on
education and writing. She serves as National Letters Chair.

(L) Janine M. DeBaise is the author of two collections of poetry,
Body Language and *Of a Feather*, published by independent presses. Her
essays have appeared in *Orion Magazine*, the *Southwest Review*, the
Hopper, and numerous other journals. She won the Vinnie Ream
Medal for her essay *The Space Between*. She teaches writing and
literature at SUNY Environmental Science and Forestry.

(A) Jeanne Dupre has enjoyed watercolor and acrylic painting for
thirty years, capturing the mood of her subject in her work. The
watercolor medium lends itself nicely to the misty mountains and
lakes she prefers as her subject. Her wish is that someone viewing
her work will stop for a few minutes and enjoy the beauty around us.

(L) Janet Clare Fagal is a retired teacher, lecturer, and award-
winning poet. Named a semi-finalist in the 2022 Vinnie Ream Medal
contest for her entry, her poems appear in *The Pen Woman*, at
NLAPW.org. in anthologies including *On Montauk, I am Someone Else*,
compiled by anthologist, Lee Bennett Hopkins, plus Pomelo
Publishing's *Great Morning!* and *Hop to It!* (2020). Janet brings poetry
into the lives and hearts of students she teaches visiting schools and
libraries.

(A) Marilyn Forth has enjoyed a distinguished career, serving as
Adjunct Professor in Textile Art at Syracuse University, lifetime
tenure with the American Craft Council shows sponsored by the
American Craft Museum, New York City. She has shown her work
in Philadelphia, Baltimore, Columbus, New York City (including the
Puck Building), as well as the Edgewood Gallery and other locations
in Syracuse.

(L) Mary Gardner poems have appeared in fourteen anthologies, including NLAPW, McMaster University, Tower Poetry Society, Syracuse Poster Project, Upstate Medical University. FootHills Publishing has published her three chapbooks of poetry. She holds a Master in Public Health from Johns Hopkins University and a Certificate in Poetry from the Syracuse Downtown Writers Center. She is a former president of the CNY Branch. In an earlier career, she published twenty articles in the health field.

(A) Wendy Harris is a nationally award-winning and collected, internationally published, multi-media painter. She is the only commissioned artist (from among eighty+ applicants) to create a 4 x 4 painting for Upstate Medical's new $74,000,000 Cancer Treatment Center, which is decorated entirely with regional art, including nine of her pieces. Her goal is to awaken everyone to the elegant, common beauty that surrounds us.

(L) Karen Foresti Hempson is a retired professor of Social Studies Education. Excerpts from her creative non-fiction book, *Bean Pickers, American Immigrant Portraits* placed as finalist in the William Faulkner-Wisdom Creative Writing Competition. It was also awarded first place in the NLAPW 2020 Biennial memoir category. Her essays have won recognition from William Faulkner Writing Competition and Vinnie Reams Writing Competition. One was published in *Pen Women Magazine*. She is currently writing an historical fiction for young adults.

(A)(L) Rachael Ikins is a multiple Pushcart nominee, CNY Book Award nominee, and 2018 Independent Book Award winner. She received fellowships to Colgate Writers Conferences and an honorarium from Finishing Line Press to read at Lismore Castle, Ireland. She is the author of six chapbooks, a full-length collection, and illustrated fantasy and mixed genre, and memoir. A prize-winning visual artist, Ikins' multi-media art appears on book covers and illustrations worldwide. An SU graduate, she is Associate Editor at Clare Songbirds Publishing House and works as a writing consultant.

(A)(L) Vanessa Johnson is a Griot, writer, playwright, actor, fiber artist, and teaching artist. Her performances, art work, and plays tell tales of Africa, the African-American experience, and of Social Justice Movements. Johnson's band *"Matie Masie"* transforms literary works into musical performances. Her program *"Griot Guides"* teaches youth the art of storytelling and provides youth with cultural exploration travel to Ghana, Africa. She is the program director for the Matilda Joslyn Gage Ambassadors for Human Rights.

(L) Maureen Teresa McCarthy has published poems and essays in *Comstock Review, Mouths to Years, Pen Woman* magazine, *Writing in a Woman's Voice, Bloom Later*, and others. Her work focuses on the natural world, imagination, and myth. She recently retired from teaching, finished a mystery novel, and is working on another novel. She has lived and written in California, Europe, Mexico, and the Finger Lakes region.

(L) Judith McGinn is a fiction writer, memoirist, and poet. She has long helped others write their memoirs through her online agency The Memoirist. Her works have appeared in *South Carolina Review, Cork Literary Review, Lun' Allure*, an anthology commemorating the 1969 moon landing, *The Brave, In the Company of Women*, and other anthologies and publications. Her short story is due to be published in 2022.

(A) Susan Murphy has always enjoyed creating art. She has shown work locally as a Signature Member of the Central New Work Watercolor Society since 1986. Her work has been accepted into the Adirondack Exhibition of American Watercolors, Cooperstown National, Niagara Frontier Watercolor Society (Creative Award), Syracuse University's Point of Contact Gallery, and the Philadelphia Water Color Society's 118 International Show. Susan recently had a solo show at Le Moyne College, Syracuse, NY.

(L) Bobbie Dumas Panek has published two books, *Morning Walks: Zen Meditations* and *Just Another Day*. Her poems appeared in aaduna.org, and moondance.org, *The Pen Woman* (NLAPW) magazine, and in the anthologies *Poems of the Super Moon, The Light Between Us, Common Intuitions, Creative Genius, Remembering Faces, Who Are You?—Self Discovery Through Journaling*, and *In the Company of Women*. Her articles have been published in *Birds and Blooms, Reminisce*

Extra, and *Many Waters* literary magazine. She is a former poetry editor of *The Pen Woman.*

(L) Georgia A. Popoff is an editor, arts-in-education specialist, faculty member and Workshops Coordinator for the YMCA of CNY'S Downtown Writers Center. She is co-author of a book for teachers on poetry in K – 12 classrooms, and co-editor of an anthology of essays on Gwendolyn Brooks. Her fourth collection of poetry, *Psychometry,* was released in 2019 by Tiger Bark Press and was a finalist for Utica College's Eugene Nassar Poetry Prize and the CNY Book Award for Poetry. Georgia received the NLAWP 2021 Vinnie Reams Award in Letters for an excerpt from her book-in-progress, *Living with Haints.*

(A) Mary Raineri is a textural artist whose abstract work straddles two and three-dimensional form. She integrates a wide variety of mixed media, including wood and fiber, metal and stone, acrylics, encaustics, inks and oils which are combined in collages and assemblages.

(A) Joan Stier is a visual artist who has made a living as an artist for the last 49 years, showing her work at festivals and other venues in Mystic, CT, King of Prussia, PA, Flemington, NJ, Buffalo, NY, Rochester, NY and in the Syracuse area. Her work consists of watercolor/ink paintings on various subjects, from the realistic to the abstract. She has won many awards, and her work is in the collections of thousands of owners.

(L) Sally Roesch Wagner is the Executive Director of The Matilda Joslyn Gage Foundation, Inc. and Gage Center for Social Justice Dialogue; an adjunct faculty member of the University Honors Program, Syracuse University; author of *We Want Equal Rights: The Haudenosaunee (Iroquois) Influence on the Women's Rights Movement,* and *Native Voices, 2020* Editor, *The Women's Suffrage Movement,* Penguin Classics, 2019. Preferred pronouns: she, her.

*(A) represents Artist members.
*(L) represents Letters members or writers in the NLAPW.